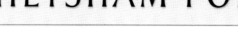

# HEYSHAM PORT

*a Century of*

Manx and Irish services

*Dick Clague*

FERRY
*Publications*

**The Mersey Docks
and Harbour Company**

# CONTENTS

## Acknowledgements

Thanks to those who have so willingly spent their time and shared their knowledge. Without them this book could not have been written: Sue Ashworth - Lancaster City Museums, Capt Stephen Carter – Laxey Towing Company, Capt John Clayton - Harbour Manager - Douglas, Miriam Critchlow - IOM Public Record Office, Capt Ken Crellin - Manx Line / IOM Steam Packet, David Dixon - Lichfield, Capt Ken Horsley - IOM Harbours, Peter Kellett - Heysham, Graham Maclean - General Manager – Heysham Port Limited, Heather McEwan – Heysham Port Limited, Chris Nolan – Seaforth Maritime Ltd, John Parkinson - Heysham, Capt Peter Reid - sometime Port Manager - Heysham, Roger Sims - Manx National Heritage, Mike Walker – Hest Bank.

We are grateful to those who have supplied their own photographs or allowed material from their own collections to be used. : Stan Basnett, M J Borrowdale, W Paul Clegg, Ian Collard, Miles Cowsill, David Dixon, David Fairclough, Ian Harmsworth, John Hendy, Dave Hocquard, Peter Joslin, Peter Kelly, John Shepherd, Peter Sunderland, Jenny Williamson, Heysham Port Limited, Lancashire West Partnership, Lancaster City Museums, Manx National Heritage, Ulster Folk and Transport Museum.

*The **Duke of Rothesay** on passage between Belfast and Heysham. (Miles Cowsill collection)*

The Midland Railway's *Manxman* going astern out of Douglas using her bow rudder. (Peter Kelly coll.)

# Foreword

Having only come to Heysham Port in 1998 I am conscious of the limits upon my knowledge of its long history. This splendid publication has changed all that. I can now reflect upon the past glories - and traumas - of this important trading gateway. I can view the development of the Port within the context of change to the broader spectrum of transport by sea, road and rail, change whose impact upon Heysham Port reflects its influence upon the wider society.

I came to Heysham not to look back but to contribute to an even stronger future for a successful port approaching a new Millennium and its own Centenary. The tide of trade and commerce has ebbed and flowed even in my short episode. In 2004 it is dramatically rising yet again, with more Irish Sea ferry sailings, expansion of general cargo and, for the first time in many a year, the mobilisation of a jack-up rig to work offshore - in this case on the Barrow windfarm site.

By far the biggest change in Heysham's fortune was the purchase of the Port in 2001 by the Mersey Docks and Harbour Company. For the first time Heysham took its place within a company whose core business was the owning and operating of ports. Substantial capital investment in both infrastructure and equipment has enabled the Port to flourish in an increasingly competitive marketplace, setting Heysham on the road to a second glorious Century.

I commend this book to anyone with an interest in not only maritime history, but also the heritage of Morecambe and Heysham. I thank the author for his diligence in researching the background information which is the bedrock of this most interesting publication.

*Captain Graham Maclean*

Capt. Graham Maclean,
General Manager,
Heysham Port.

# Introduction

The Midland Railway port of Heysham opened to traffic in 1904 – a new port built on reclaimed land where there had been no previous harbour. Whilst the main purpose of this book is to celebrate the centenary of the Port of Heysham, this also requires reference to the major services and ships which have operated to the Isle of Man, Belfast, Dublin and (more recently) to Warrenpoint. It is also important to see how those services have impinged on the growth of their ports. Most recently, there has been the additional development of the gas field support base within the confines of Heysham Harbour.

None of the Irish Sea routes from Heysham have operated continuously for the century under review but, apart from Londonderry and Portrush, all the ports served in the first year of operation are still served now, with the addition of the route to Warrenpoint. Most routes, apart from that to the Isle of Man, are now freight-only although there was a brief resumption of Belfast passenger sailings on a seasonal basis between 1999 and 2002.

I am particularly grateful to all those who have spent generously of their time in providing me with information, photographs and encouragement. Without them this book could not have been written – their names are listed at the end of the book but I would particularly thank Heysham Port Limited and Mersey Docks & Harbour Company for sponsoring the book as well as Captain Ken

*Laird Lines' **Hazel** – later sold to the IOM Steam Packet and re-named the **Mona**. (Courtesy of Manx National Heritage)*

Crellin who has sailed in and out of Heysham as Master for over 25 years, and has contributed the chapter on "Sailing the Douglas – Heysham Route".

## The main operating companies at Heysham

Until Heysham Port opened in 1904, the Midland Railway's Irish Sea shipping interests had been through their investment in the Barrow Steam Navigation Company – in which their partners were the

*The **Manx Viking** in her original Manx Line colours going astern from the Victoria Pier as she sets out for Heysham. (Stan Basnett)*

*The **Duke of Argyll** going astern in Belfast Lough.(Ferry Publications Library)*

Furness Railway and James Little. The BSNC ships were all transferred to Midland Railway ownership in 1907.

In 1923 there was a major re-organisation of railway companies which led to the formation of the LMS (London Midland & Scottish Railway) which absorbed the Midland Railway as well as the London & North Western and Lancashire and Yorkshire Railways which operated Irish services from Fleetwood.

When the railways were nationalised in 1948 to form British Railways (known as British Rail from 1964), the Irish Sea services formed part of the London Midland Region.

Eventually all the railway shipping interests were put into a separate operating group – the Shipping & International Services Division (S.I.S.D.) which adopted the Sealink brand name in late 1969. The Sealink operation, including the port of Heysham, was sold to Sea Containers in 1984. The sale included Sealink-Manx Line which had been established in 1978. When the Swedish operator Stena Line took over most of the Sealink operation in 1990, Heysham and Sealink-Manx Line were excluded.

The Isle of Man Steam Packet Company (formed in 1830) was already well established on the Liverpool and Fleetwood routes to the Isle of Man when it took over the Heysham service from the LMS in 1928. Following the Steam Packet merger with Sealink-Manx Line in 1985, Sea Containers took a 40% shareholding in the combined company, taking total control in 1996.

Sea Containers eventually sold Heysham Port Limited to Mersey Docks and Harbour Company in 2001 and the Isle of Man Steam Packet Company to Montagu Private Equity in 2003.

Laird Line, whose primary trade was between Scotland and Ireland, operated Irish services from Heysham between 1904 and 1963. They had merged with G&J Burns to form Burns & Laird Lines in 1922. This company was to be controlled by Coast Lines Ltd and eventually absorbed into the P&O Group.

NorseMerchant Ferries (formed in 2001) operates to Belfast and Dublin and incorporates Belfast Freight Ferries (formed in 1984) and Merchant Ferries which started in 1986. Seatruck Ferries, which have operated to Warrenpoint since 1996 are part of the Danish Clipper group.

Dick Clague
May 2004

# Building the Port of Heysham

## Why the port was needed.

The Lancashire coastline has few natural harbours, and where these exist the approach channels have been subject to silting and shipping operations tidally constrained. Even when piers were built in places like Blackpool and Southport they were too exposed for anything other than fair weather seasonal use. During the later part of the 19th century the private and fiercely competitive railway companies had not only extended their rail networks on land but had established shipping services from their railheads to Ireland and the Isle of Man. Around the British coastline this was ultimately to lead to the development of many "railway ports" including Harwich, Dover, Folkestone, Newhaven, Fishguard, Holyhead, Heysham and Stranraer - although other ports were also used for railway services. The biggest port owner was the North Eastern Railway, which made it the more surprising that the commercially aggressive Midland Railway had no port of its own. Brunel's vision for the Great Western Railway led him into shipbuilding so that their services could be extended beyond Bristol and Plymouth to North America.

During the latter part of the 19th century, Irish services had operated from Morecambe, using tidally constrained facilities built in 1853 by the North Western Railway (not to be confused with the London & North Western Railway), which was finally taken over in 1871 by the Midland Railway. Despite considerable port improvements in 1855 and 1859 there was no possibility of running fixed time schedules. No local solution to these problems being possible, the Midland Railway then joined forces with the Furness Railway transferring its passenger operations to Piel Pier at Barrow in 1867 and its freight and cargo operations to Barrow Docks which by then were owned by the Furness Railway. This led to the formation of the Barrow Steam Navigation Company [BSNC] the following year in

*The Londonderry and Belfast sheds on the South Quay were erected at quite an early stage. – before the Harbour was flooded in February 1904. (Heysham Port collection)*

which the two railway companies were joined by James Little - each holding equal shares. In 1885 services were transferred from Piel Pier to the newly constructed Ramsden Dock at Barrow which had its own railway station for connecting trains. The BSNC ran services both to the Isle of Man and to Northern Ireland.

Although there had been regular steamer sailings from Fleetwood from 1841 onwards the operators and services offered varied from year to year and the facilities were inadequate to make the connecting rail services economic. In 1870 the Lancashire & Yorkshire Railway and the London & North Western Railway obtained joint powers to own and run their own ships from Fleetwood and in 1877 opened the new dock there which had taken over four years to build. Services from Fleetwood were then firmly established both to Ireland and the Isle of Man, and a new well-equipped passenger station was opened in 1883. The travel time from London to Belfast via Fleetwood was 12 hours 45 minutes in contrast to 16 hours via Barrow, thus leaving the Midland Railway at a considerable competitive disadvantage.

## Early plans

The only solution for the Midland Railway was to come back to Morecambe Bay – where it had access over its own tracks – and so it was to the Heysham area it looked to construct a completely new port. Heysham lies on the Lancashire coast at Latitude 54° 02' N and Longitude 2° 55' W. It is about 3 miles south of Morecambe and there is a tongue of deep-water (with access to the open sea) known as Heysham Lake, about 3/4 mile from the headlands of Near Naze and Far Naze. This area had been looked at as early as 1864 and progressed to the point of a Heysham Pier and Railway Bill being passed the following year - but no port development had ever materialised. In

*The Fish Quay is taking shape on the left of this picture and the North Quay can be seen further away to the right. (Heysham Port collection)*

1891 the Midland Railway gave notice of its intention to develop a new harbour at Heysham and appointed as Consulting Engineers James Abernethy and his son (George Neil Abernethy) to undertake a full feasibility study of the project. Despite an enabling Bill being passed the next year, this plan - which was for an enclosed dock with access through a lock - made no further progress.

An Abernethy breakwater had already been built in Douglas at the suggestion of the Admiralty in 1864. This was a timber-framed construction with stone infill which was intended to protect the mouth of the inner harbour. It proved inadequate for the task being partially demolished by a SE storm in 1865 and two years later another gale finished the job off. What Abernethy was to propose for Heysham was a good deal more substantial and stood the test of time.

*The construction of the roundhead is clearly visible on the left hand side of this picture in the early stages of construction of Heysham Harbour. (Heysham Port collection)*

## The 1895 scheme

In 1895 a much larger Heysham scheme was put forward by Messrs James Abernethy & Son in conjunction with the Midland Railway's chief engineer J Allen McDonald and this formed the basis of the harbour which was actually built – although there were to be many changes as work progressed and the full scheme was never completed. The 1895 scheme proposed a tidal harbour enclosed by two breakwaters. In 1896 an enabling Act was obtained for the construction of the harbour and, after the death of James Abernethy, his son George Neil Abernethy was appointed with J Allen McDonald as Joint Engineer for the project. Following detail design work the contact for the construction of the harbour was let in July 1897 to Price & Wills of Westminster. The project cost approximately £3 million.

The plan was to build two curved breakwaters out into Morecambe Bay, one from the rocky promontories of Near Naze and another from Red Nab, the landward end of the breakwaters being a little over a mile apart. The seaward ends of the two breakwaters would be nearly half a mile from the original shoreline and form a harbour entrance 91.4 metres wide. From this entrance it was about 275 metres to the deep water of Heysham Lake. Apart from the area required for the tidal harbour, the rest of the enclosed area would be infilled to the height of

11

the breakwaters, although space had been provided for the development of a larger enclosed dock on the southern part of the site. Within the tidal harbour the original proposal had been for a 275 metres long x 46metres wide central pier with its own railway station for handling passengers and cattle – but this was eliminated from the design in 1900 before its construction began.

## The construction phase

The first stage of the project was to build enclosing embankments along the line of the seaward side of the projected breakwaters. These were formed by excavating the cliffs at the back of the site and sandstone blocks were then put on the seaward side of these new embankments. George Abernethy later described the construction:

"A trench was first cut in the sand and filled with sandstone rock to form a toe, and to prevent erosion by the sea; two rock tips were then started on each embankment, the space between the tips being filled with clay and marl; but later on, and after getting further seaward, it was found better and more expeditious to tip a single rock bank from two lines of rails and to side tip the clay and marl on the inner face".

This work started in the later part of 1897 and by April 1899 the external boundaries were secured from the sea and a temporary rock faced clay dam with a 1.8 metre diameter pipe with a sluice had been built across what was to be the harbour mouth. During construction a 91.5 metre timber viaduct had been inserted to allow the tide to flow in and out but once the rest of the work had been done this was infilled with rock.

One of the problems of Morecambe Bay is quicksand and, as the work developed seawards, it became apparent that a rock filled trench in the sand formed an inadequate foundation. This problem was

*Dredgers at work in the harbour shortly after the breakthrough had been made into Morecambe Bay early in 1904. (Heysham Port collection)*

overcome by casting 7.3 metre long concrete monolith blocks on which brick walls were built. These blocks would sink under their own weight as the brick walls were built, subsidence as much as 1.5 metres in a day being reported. A similar technique was used to build the two roundheads at the harbour entrance. These were 16.5 metres in diameter, 2.4 metres deep and weighed 73 tons each. The northern monolith sank 23 metres before reaching solid rock and over 1 million bricks were then used in building it up. The resulting structures are estimated to weigh around 6,000 tons each.

To provide access to the site – and later the new port – a railway branch line from Morecambe was constructed without difficulty and opened on 1st November 1898. In addition the contractors were to lay

*Each harbour-mouth roundhead was 16.75 metres in diameter. Over a million bricks were used to build them up as they sank nearly 23 metres through the sand to the rock below, the complete structures weighing around 6,000 tonnes each. (Heysham Port collection)*

16 miles of temporary track during the course of the project and had their own fleet of 20 locomotives, 600 tip and side wagons and 180 ballast trucks. For maintaining this system and the other civil engineering equipment on the construction site they had a fitting shop and brass foundry, saw mills and a carpenters' shed. There were engine sheds and even a paint shop. Estimates of the number of men employed on the project vary between 700 and 2000 and to house them two hutted camps were used which were known as "Klondike" and "Dawson City". These were remarkably complete communities with their own shops, police station, schools and hospitals.

Once the site was pumped dry, excavation within the harbour started. Much of the material taken out was used to widen the

breakwater embankments. Abernethy reported that: "in the first instance they were 9.1 metres in width at the top and the material was side tipped until a width of 183 metres at the root and 52 metres at the ends was obtained. It was then found advisable to heighten the outer embankment from 3 to 4.3 metres above high water of ordinary spring tides as a further protection against storms and extraordinarily high tides. The original proposal was for a depth of water within the harbour of 2.1 metres below low-water of ordinary spring tides, but subsequently this was increased to 4.3 metres."

After excavation of the harbour basin it was intended to build the quay walls above timber framed trenches but it was found that the ground was firm enough for this not to be necessary and the

*The interior of the Heysham Harbour Power Station in 1908. (Courtesy of Lancaster City Museums)*

13

*The original Heysham station before the line was electrified in 1908. (Courtesy of Lancaster City Museums)*

*Construction of the harbour began in 1897. (John Walker-Courtesy of Lancaster City Museums)*

foundations were dug as part of the general excavation. As built the South Quay is 1600 ft long, the North Quay 275 metres and the Fish Quay 91.5 metres. The east end of the harbour and the section between the North Quay and the Fish Quay are faced with rock slopes. The South Quay was built to be able to handle up to five passenger/cattle steamers at any stage of the tide. It is 16.2 metres high and was originally faced with a three-level wooden (Australian Karri) staging which connected with stairs, cattle subways and covered pedestrian bridges. Whilst this staging has long since fallen into disuse for its intended purpose, relics of it still remain at the seaward end of the South Quay 100 years later. The shorter North Quay was of similar construction but without the staging.

Provision was also made for the building of a lock in the south-west corner of the harbour. The entrance walls of the lock were built and then bricked up. This would have provided access to the enclosed dock which was never built.

By September 1903 all the excavations and the new harbour walls were completed so the contractors were able to flood the harbour by opening the sluice in the temporary dam. Sand pump dredgers had already started work on forming the short channel between the harbour entrance and Heysham Lake and as the water rose the next job was to demolish the temporary dam to low water level. By 16th February 1904 dredgers were able to enter the new harbour at high water and by May the channel was dredged to full depth and all trace

A 1908 view of the cattle sidings taken from the Harbour Power Station. (Courtesy of Lancaster City Museums)

The South Jetty under construction in 1909 to reduce silting of the harbour entrance. (Courtesy of Lancaster City Museums)

of the temporary dam had gone. The 36 acre harbour was virtually complete but there were still problems to be overcome with the new entrance channel which was requiring virtually continuous dredging. The solution suggested was to build two stone groynes on either side of the channel, but these proved of little help as they sank without trace into the sands of Morecambe Bay. Powers to build two further jetties - one from each roundhead - were obtained in 1907 but only the South Jetty was actually built.

## Port facilities

The construction work ashore was considerable. It had been decided that the port and railway station would have their own power supply so not only was a power station built to generate electricity - 100 years later the building still in use as a workshop standing on a traffic island in the port approaches - but also a coal fired gas plant to power it. As virtually all of the port equipment was to be electrically powered, accumulators were installed to provide a reserve of at least 6 hours supply. Heysham was the first UK port to be built with all-electric plant. The port also had its own water supply which came from an artesian well which fed into a reservoir.

A small lighthouse was built on the southern roundhead but electricity was not considered a suitable means of illumination, gas being used with a two-wick oil burner as standby. The lighthouse structure itself was built with cast iron plates and bolted down by 16

*The **Duchess of Devonshire** in her original BSNC colours. (Peter Kelly collection)*

A passenger station and two goods sheds were built on the South Quay. In the 'Railway Magazine' of November 1904. W F Nokes wrote: "Deserving of mention is the passenger station at Heysham, affording as it does every convenience for all classes of travellers. The platform is of the island type, and, besides the booking office, has refreshment and waiting rooms of the usual grades. An overhead lift for luggage enables the passenger to obtain a glance of his impedimenta as he emerges from the bridge connecting platform and quay".

The station, which was replaced in 1968 and demolished in 1972, was covered by a roof 137 metres long and 23 metres wide - the platform being 183 metres long. Between the station and the quay was the Belfast Goods shed - a 152 metre long building over which enclosed passenger walkways were constructed. A smaller goods shed (53.3 metres long) was constructed further up the harbour to handle the Londonderry cargo. All these buildings were wooden clad steel frame constructions with 1 in 2 inclined roofs to minimise wind resistance - the site being particularly

bolts of 1.5 inch diameter and 6 ft length. A second light was erected on a four column iron tower on the Naze Rocks and this acted as a leading light in conjunction with the lighthouse for guiding ships up Heysham Lake. Both lighthouses were supplied and erected by Chance Bros. of Birmingham.

exposed in SW gales. As well as the railway tracks going into the station and goods sheds, another line was laid along the quayside under the dockside cranes. There were also extensive sidings on both sides of the harbour.

The North Quay was designated for general cargo handling and business was by no means restricted to Irish Sea destinations or the Midland Railway's ships. Extensive open hard standing was available behind the quay and this was used for iron ore, pig iron, slates and timber storage. The Fish Quay was never used for its intended purpose as the major Lancashire fishing fleets saw no benefit in moving from their established facilities in Fleetwood and even more-local fishermen based at Morecambe showed little interest in relocating their base.

Livestock movements from Ireland were a major trade during the first half of the 20th century and one of the unusual features of the port was the provision of paddocks for both cattle and geese. It was recognised that animals might suffer during the sea passage from Ireland, but that their value might be enhanced if they were able to recuperate before being sent to the English markets. The Regulations and Schedules of the Port of Heysham state that: "A portion of the Harbour is an authorised Landing Place for Irish animals, and extensive accommodation is afforded for resting, feeding and grazing cattle and other live stock. Horses, cattle and other live stock are landed by means of sloping ways, so no slinging is necessary. Slaughterhouses, sheep dipping tank, etc., are provided".

## The port opens

The first major ship to dock at Heysham was the *Antrim* one of four new buildings the Midland Railway had ordered for their Heysham services. She came into the harbour on delivery from her

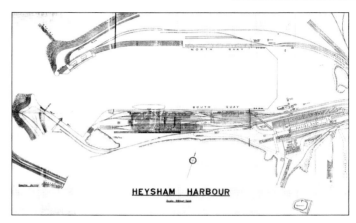

*Heysham Habour after the Second World War. (Courtesy of Lancaster City Museums)*

builders, John Brown, at Clydebank on 31st May 1904. The first passenger sailing was a day trip to Douglas by the *Londonderry* on 13th August 1904 and this was followed by a number of local cruises. This ship also made the first sailing to Belfast on 25th August carrying the Midland Railway's directors and the *Antrim* followed two days later with a special excursion for those who had built the ship. The first regular scheduled sailing was taken by the *Antrim* sailing to Belfast on 1st September 1904. The Laird Line vessel *Shamrock* had arrived light from Morecambe the previous day and took their first sailing to Dublin. The port of Heysham was open for business.

*Douglas Harbour around 1900. Passenger traffic was mainly handled at the far pier (Victoria Pier). It was not until the 1930s the tidal Red Pier (with lighthouse) was extended to provide all tide berthing. (Photo courtesy of Manx National Heritage)*

# PORTS SERVED FROM HEYSHAM

By the time Heysham Port opened in 1904, Belfast and Douglas, the two ports with which its Midland Railway services were to be linked, were already well established. Dublin, to be served initially by Laird Lines, was even longer established but Warrenpoint – which was not to see regular services to Heysham until 80 years later - was still in private ownership.

## Douglas

Douglas had already been a recognisable harbour for more than a century before the IOM Steam Packet started operations in 1830. The original working harbour was the area above the lift bridge which

*A similar view of Douglas Harbour taken in 2003. (Author's photo)*

dried out completely at low tide. Old pictures show cargo being lowered over the side of ships into horse- drawn carts standing on the dried out harbour bed. The earliest recognisable quay was probably built around 1700 at the top of today's inner harbour. This was of no benefit to passengers who were landed from boats anchored in the bay, usually at the small pier on the Pollock Rocks - the remains of which protrude into the bay from the base of the Victoria Pier.

The need for sheltered landing facilities had long been apparent but no effort was made to extend the harbour seawards until the Red Pier was completed in 1801. This was a 168 metre extension of the North Quay - reaching about as far as the line of the overhead section of the passenger walkway to the King Edward pier. It gave limited protection to the harbour entrance but only provided tidal berths. It provided no shelter at all in SE gales. In 1829 Sir William Hilary (founder of the RNLI), supported by a number of Liverpool ship owners who complained of the number of wrecks which had taken place in the vicinity of Douglas harbour, persuaded the Admiralty to send a commissioner to assess the situation. Proposals were made but nothing was done. It was from these meagre facilities that the Isle of Man Steam Packet started operation in 1830. In 1835 Sir John Rennie drew up a major scheme, of which only the Fort Anne Jetty was built as a breakwater for the inner harbour. His plans were reconsidered in 1839, 1840 and 1846 but no money was available. In 1846 and 1853 the IOM Harbour Commissioners failed to get backing to build a masonry breakwater and in 1858 the Royal Commission on Harbours of Refuge drew up a £100,000 scheme - but again no funding was forthcoming.

Douglas Harbour is owned by the Manx Government who, despite various flirtations with the idea, does not own any shipping operations.

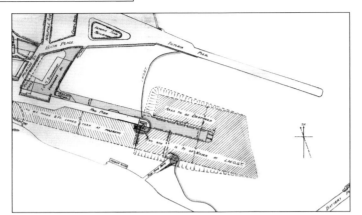

*A 1908 plan of Douglas Harbour, showing the proposed Red Pier extension not built until the 1930's. (Author's collection)*

Harbour users are its commercial customers and much of the history of Douglas harbour arises from the fluctuating relationships between the Harbour authority and its main users. At the turn of the 21st Century all Manx Harbours were controlled by the Harbours Division of the Department of Transport, successors to the Isle of Man Harbour Board and before that the Isle of Man Harbour Commissioners.

Throughout its history there have been two main issues in tension - the need to provide more (or different types of) berthing facilities and the need to provide better shelter for the harbour. The tension arises because the creation of increased/improved berthing has often required better shelter - but the funds have rarely been available to finance both simultaneously. An inability to resolve this tension has led to beneficial schemes being delayed for decades, and, where improvements have

been effected without adequate shelter, great difficulties have ensued. It is probably only since the construction of the Princess Alexandra Breakwater (opened in 1983) that shelter has become adequate for the operation of the harbour in almost all weather conditions.

### Belfast

The first port authority for Belfast – the Ballast Board – was established in 1785. Its full title was "The Corporation for preserving and improving the Port and Harbour of Belfast". A recognisable port had however been in existence since 1613, when a Royal Charter, in which the town was incorporated as a borough, made provision for the establishment of the first quay which was subsequently constructed at the confluence of the rivers Lagan and Fearset.

*Belfast's Donegall Quay – the departure point for most of the steamers to England and Scotland. Taken between 1912 and 1914. (National Museums and Galleries of Northern Ireland, Ulster Folk & Transport Museum)*

The first steamer arrival was the paddle steamer *Greenock* in 1816 from the Clyde via Campbeltown and Bangor. The approach to the quays was up the winding River Lagan and the first cut to straighten the river was opened in 1841. The Belfast Harbour Commissioners took over the role of trustees of the Port of Belfast in 1847 and in 1849 the Victoria Channel was opened, finally giving a straight approach to the port from Belfast Lough. The same year the timber faced Donegall Quay – which was to be the base for cross-Channel steamers - was built, but it was also rebuilt with stone facing in two sections in 1879-80 and 1882-86 and extended in 1885/88. There was also a separate jetty adjacent to Donegall Quay and accessed from the Queens Bridge from which local steamers to Bangor ran.

As the port developed and the size of ships increased further

*A Seatruck Ferries vessel leaving Warrenpoint for Heysham. (Alistair Eagles)*

dredging was required to increase the depth of water in the Victoria Channel – major work being undertaken in 1886-1891 to extend it seaward by 6 kilometres and to deepen it in 1898-1900.

## Dublin

Dublin and Heysham were linked by Laird Lines' services (usually six days a week) from 1904 until 1926 and, more recently, by NorseMerchant Ferries (previously Merchant Ferries) since 1995. The Port of Dublin traces its origins back to the 9th Century but the "Ballast Committee" was only established to maintain and develop the port in 1708. They were responsible for the building of the Great South Wall (1786) and the North Bull Wall (1824) which protect the harbour entrance from siltation to this day. At the time Heysham port opened in 1904 the working area of Dublin Port was almost entirely upriver of the East Link Toll Bridge. The port developed steadily seawards through the 20th Century with the ro-ro terminal at Alexandra Road Extension, now used by NorseMerchant Ferries, opening on reclaimed land in 1995.

## Warrenpoint

Warrenpoint stands at the head of Carlingford Lough on the Northern Ireland side of the border with the Irish Republic. A wet dock and piers were constructed there in the late 1770s, the port's main purpose being for seagoing vessels to transfer their cargoes to lighters for onward shipment upriver to Newry. The Warrenpoint Harbour Authority purchased the port from private owners in 1971 and established container handling facilities as well as building a single ro-ro ramp from which Merchant Ferries opened services to Heysham in 1985.

# A Century of Operations

## 1904 – 1918.

### Services from Heysham

Not only had the Midland Railway invested heavily in building the port of Heysham, it also invested in four new purpose- built ships. All were designed by one of the leading naval architects of the time Sir John Biles, Professor of Naval Architecture at Glasgow University, and delivered during 1904 from four different yards.

The *Antrim* and the *Donegal* , whilst being by no means identical, could be classed as sister ships having twin screws and triple-expansion engines. The *Londonderry* was mechanically different having triple screws and Parsons steam turbines – but was of similar dimensions (100.6 x 12.8 metres). All were built on the Clyde, but by three different yards (John Brown, Caird, and Denny). All three were fitted out for the overnight Heysham – Belfast service. The *Manxman* was slightly longer and beamier and was built for the day traffic to the Isle of Man by Vickers Sons & Maxim at Barrow. She too was a triple-screwed turbine steamer but had larger turbines and her boilers worked at higher pressure than any previous turbine steamer – 200 psi (pounds per square inch) compared to the *Londonderry*'s 150 – giving her a service speed of 22 knots. As the first

commercial turbine steamer in the world (the *King Edward*) had only been launched on the Clyde in 1901 the *Londonderry* and *Manxman* were very much state of the art mechanically. All four ships were fitted with radio and the Midland Railway built a wireless telegraph station on ground between the South Quay and South breakwater at Heysham to keep in touch with its fleet.

The Belfast service opened on 1st September 1904, running to Donegall Quay. It had always been intended that the Isle of Man service would be seasonal, so after delivery in November 1904, the *Manxman* initially acted as relief ship on the Belfast run. Her maiden voyage to Douglas was not until 1st June 1905. She was commanded by Captain Hill who had been Marine Superintendent of the IOM Steam Packet Co until "poached" by the Midland Railway for a higher salary – which the Steam Packet board did not offer to match. The usual pattern of working on the Belfast service was for each ship to run for a month and then lay up for 15 days in Heysham, except for peak season Saturdays, when the "spare boat" would be used to supplement the Isle of Man service. The *Manxman* was usually in Douglas overnight.

The *Duchess of Devonshire* had been delivered to the Barrow Steam Navigation Company in 1897 and had been taken over by the Midland Railway. She was built as a dual-purpose ship to run Barrow – IOM in summer and to act as relief ship for Barrow – Belfast in winter. Her cabins could be removed when she was on the IOM service. Once Heysham services were established she saw little winter service and was usually laid up with the *Manxman* at Barrow in winter. Being considerably slower than the *Manxman*, she had a service speed of 19 knots – but still slightly faster than the *Ben-my-Chree* [6] which was to work the route 100 years later. The peak

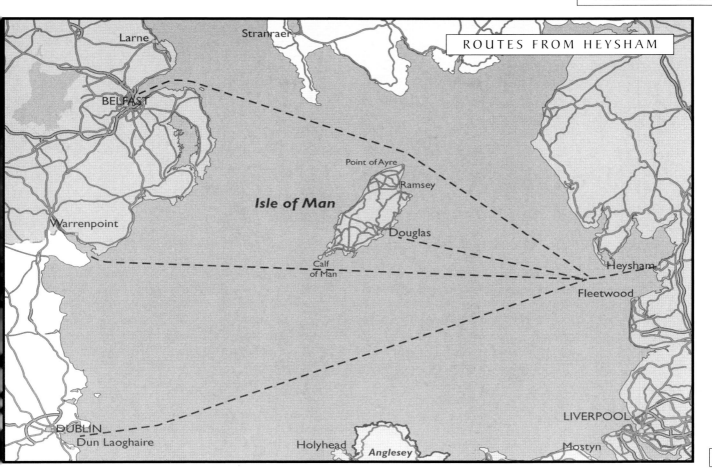

*An early photograph of the Midland Railway's* **Londonderry** *arriving at Heysham. (Courtesy of Lancaster City Museums)*

The **Manxman** *passes the ever-needed dredger as she arrives at Heysham prior to 1910. (Courtesy of Lancaster City Museums)*

Saturday services to the Isle of Man were often considerably augmented and on occasion some of the older Barrow ships were pressed into service. In 1907 all the Midland's Heysham ships visited Douglas at some time and the *Duchess of Buccleuch* (still a regular visitor from Barrow) and the *City of Belfast* were also occasionally used on the route.

W F Nokes ('Railway Magazine' - Nov 1904) wrote of the Midland steamers that "no additional charge is made for sleeping accommodation on the steamers; each passenger on presentation of his ticket to the purser is allotted a suitable cabin or berth, the Midland Railway discouraging as far as possible passengers sleeping in the saloons which menaces the comfort of others who do not care to sleep at sea on cross-Channel passages". Single cabins were apparently available on payment of a premium of 2/6 (12.5p).

**Heysham – Dublin – Heysham**
service by:   Laird Line steamer
*Daily service*

| Leeds dep | 17.40 | Dublin dep | 19.30 |
|---|---|---|---|
| Heysham arr | 20.40 | Heysham arr | |
| Heysham dep | 21.00 | Heysham dep | 07.30 |
| Dublin (North Wall) arr | 07.00 | Leeds arr | |

**Heysham – Belfast – Heysham**
service by: *Antrim, Donegal, Londonderry*
*Daily service*

| St Pancras dep | 18.00 | Belfast dep | 21.30 |
|---|---|---|---|
| Heysham arr | 23.52 | Heysham arr | 05.40 |
| Heysham dep | 00.05 | Heysham dep | 06.15 |
| Belfast (Donegal Quay)arr | 06.20 | St Pancras arr | |
| Belfast dep | 08.00 | | |
| (to Portrush / Londonderry) | | | |

**Heysham – Londonderry – Heysham**
service by: Laird Line steamer
to Londonderry          Wed and Sat only
from Londonderry       Tues and Fri only

| St Pancras dep | 18.00 | Londonderry dep | 15.30 |
|---|---|---|---|
| Heysham arr | 23.52 | Heysham arr | |
| Heysham dep | 00.00 | Heysham dep | 07.30 |
| Londonderry arr | | Leeds arr | |

**Heysham – Douglas – Heysham**
summer service only
service by     *Manxman, Duchess of Devonshire*

| Heysham dep | 15.00 | Heysham dep | 10.00 |
|---|---|---|---|
| Douglas arr | 17.45 | Douglas arr | 13.15 |
| Douglas dep | 09.30 | Douglas dep | 16.00 |
| Heysham arr | 12.15 | Heysham arr | 19.30 |

rail connections to
London, Birmingham, Harrogate

Another innovation on the Belfast steamers was the introduction of a number of 4 berth cabins for steerage passengers.

Laird Line switched their Morecambe services to Heysham immediately the new port opened – daily to Dublin and twice weekly to Londonderry. Unlike the Midland Railway, Laird Line used many different ships on what were referred to as their "outport services" from Heysham. In 1905 the *Olive* and *Thistle* were usually on the Dublin run (which the *Shamrock* had opened the previous year) and the *Brier* and *Azalea* served Londonderry with a call en route at Portrush. By 1909 the *Hazel* (later sold to the Steam Packet as the *Mona*) appeared on their rosters.

Although Heysham port was now open there was still a serious problem with silting in the final approach channel. This was partly due to the tidal flow across the harbour mouth and partly due to the failure of the stone retaining groynes which had sunk into the quicksand. In July 1907 it was reported that "The difficulties with regard to keeping the harbour and channel open at Heysham still exist. On a recent visit I found that in addition to the large steaming bucket dredger belonging to the Midland Company, and the two steam hoppers that wait upon it, there were at work a steaming suction dredger and steaming bucket dredger with two attendant steam hoppers. This fleet is constantly at work at low water and I believe there has been very little or no change in the number of dredgers etc since the harbour was opened". Parliamentary powers to build two further jetties - one from each roundhead - were obtained in 1907 but only the South Jetty was actually built, work starting in 1909 and being completed in 1911.

By 1913 the pattern of ship and boat train working which had emerged was as illustrated on the left.

round trips each day providing excursions for holidaymakers in the Lancaster/Morecambe area through to Blackpool – using the connecting trains from Fleetwood.

Her other duties were described by Captain Alf Willmott who was Harbour Master at Heysham during her final years of service "In poor visibility and fog, she stationed herself at no 3 (later no 6) buoy … and sounded 6 short blasts on the steam whistle to guide the approaching inward bound mail vessel. When she had been visually sighted the *Wyvern* proceeded to the harbour entrance buoy and made the same signal to guide the mail vessel to the harbour entrance. This operation could only be carried out at Low Water slack; duration two and a half hours; and for a limited period of

*The tug/tender **Wyvern** served at Heysham between 1905 and 1959. For many years she operated a seasonal passenger service between Heysham and Fleetwood.(Ian Harmsworth)*

Mention must also be made of the *Wyvern*. She was a twin screw tug which was built by Ferguson at Port Glasgow as a tender to assist the mail steamers in Heysham Harbour. She operated from 1905 until 1959 and, until 1957, held a passenger certificate for 230. Apart from her towage and tendering duties she operated a passenger service between Heysham Harbour and Fleetwood from the end of June to the end of September. The trip was scheduled for one hour in each direction but could be accomplished in 40 minutes. In the early days of the Heysham operation the *Wyvern* was also used to collect Isle of Man passengers from Fleetwood and bring them to Heysham in time to catch the Midland steamer. Apart from the war years 1914 - 1918 this service ran from 1905 until 1939 with two

*The Midland Railway's **Donegal** alongside Heysham's South Quay before the First World War. She was sunk by a U-boat in 1917.(John Hendy collection)*

about 20 minutes at High Water slack". She was also used to make the annual pilotage trips which all Heysham Masters and some officers were required to make to Fleetwood as Heysham was part of the Fleetwood pilotage area. Her towage duties included assisting in the refloating on 4th October 1908 of the *Donegal* after she had gone ashore near the Point of Ayre (Isle of Man). Captain Willmott noted also that "she had assisted the mail vessels whenever they grounded outside the (Heysham) harbour".

By 1913 the peak summer trade to the Isle of Man had built up to the level that on Saturday 9th August the following sailings took place - the only Heysham ship not being used being the *Donegal* which was in Belfast:

**Heysham – Douglas**

| a.m. | light | *Londonderry* |
|---|---|---|
| 10.00 | | *Duchess of Devonshire* |
| 11.30 | | *Antrim* |
| 15.00 | | *Manxman* |
| 24.00 | | *Duchess of Devonshire* |

**Douglas – Heysham**

| 08.30 | | *Manxman* |
|---|---|---|
| 09.30 | | *Londonderry* |
| 15.00 | | *Manxman* |
| 16.00 | | *Duchess of Devonshire* |
| evening | | *Londonderry* |

Notes: The *Antrim* was the Belfast service boat which arrived Heysham at 05.40. The *Londonderry* was the spare ship that weekend.

## Railway connections

It was also noted that several special trains had to be run to accommodate the large number of passengers involved. At this time there were frequent local electric trains to Morecambe and Lancaster but the majority of passengers would have arrived on the special boat trains. Heysham - like other railway ports of the period - was built on the basis that all passengers and freight would arrive by train and virtually no provision was made for road access to the port.

Important to the Midland Railway as the ships were, they were but part of an integrated transport system to enable passengers to be transported from major towns in England to Ireland and the Isle of Man. A boat train would leave London's St Pancras station at 17.00 each weekday calling at Kettering, Nottingham, Sheffield and Leeds, arriving at Heysham at 22.45 in time for passengers to catch the 23.00 sailing. The 15-minute connection time between arrival of the train and departure of the steamer was no problem when both were operated by the same company. The return boat train (to connect with the 21.00 departure from Belfast) left Heysham for London at 05.20 taking 6 hours to reach St Pancras. A contemporary report mentions that it was "furnished with a breakfast car, deterring passengers from developing unnecessary ferociousness ere they reach their destination".

By 1907 the line from Lancaster (Green Ayre) to Morecambe and Heysham was so heavily used that it was decided to electrify it and a 20 minute frequency service was introduced from 1st July 1908. This was extended to Lancaster (Castle) 3 months later. This was the first A/C railway electrification in the UK and power was supplied from the Heysham Harbour power station which was increased in size for the purpose.

*The Midland Railway's **Manxman** going astern from the Victoria Pier en route for Heysham. Two IOM Steam Packet paddle steamers are lying at the Battery Pier. (Courtesy of Manx National Heritage*

*Laird Line's **Hazel** and the Midland Railway's **Antrim** at Heysham in May 1909. Both ships were ultimately bought by the IOM Steam Packet and re-named **Mona** and **Ramsey Town** respectively. (Courtesy of Lancaster City Museums)*

## The problem at Douglas

Whilst the Midland Railway had state-of-the-art facilities in Heysham the real growth in its business was on the Manx route, with the Belfast "night" steamers often being pressed into day sailings to the Isle of Man to meet peak weekend traffic. Douglas Harbour's two main problems were lack of shelter – particularly during NE gales – and insufficient all-tide berths. The Battery Pier had been built as a breakwater designed by Sir John Coode and opened in 1879 but passenger vessels used the Victoria Pier, built in 1867-72 and lengthened by 120 metres in 1887-91. This was then able to accommodate four ships at all states of the tide but was very exposed in bad weather.

Trade continued to grow, helped by the aggressive marketing of the Midland's new service from Heysham. Through fares for rail and sea travel were agreed through the Railway Clearing House. The Midland Railway gave notice in August 1904 that on its new Heysham - IOM route it wished to undercut the excursion fares offered by the Lancashire & Yorkshire Railway in conjunction with Steam Packet via Fleetwood. The Manx company naturally opposed the move but when the Midland persisted they had to decide, in conjunction with their railway partners, whether to match the new lower fares. The day return fare proposed by the Midland for 1905 was 5/- (25p) First Class and 3/- (15p) – in each case a reduction of 1/- (5p). Period returns were double this.

As the competition was successfully leading to an increase in business, the shipping operators were clamouring for even more berths in Douglas from which to land their passengers. Schemes were put forward in 1904, 1908 and 1914 to extend the original Red Pier but, as the 1905 Report to Tynwald (the Isle of Man's parliament) put it: the "advantage likely to be derived from their construction not being sufficient to justify the imposition of fresh taxation" they came to naught. In consequence double and sometimes triple berthing of vessels was quite frequent with the seven ships due to arrive on peak Saturday afternoons only having four berths available.

During the first week of August 1907, 107 passenger steamers arrived at the Victoria Pier (in 1885 the number had been 66) and on the busiest day 36,127 passengers were landed. That season the Steam Packet had a fleet of twelve passenger ships. Their main routes were to Liverpool and Fleetwood but there were also regular sailings to Ardrossan, Belfast and Dublin and occasional sailings to Garliestown, Glasgow and Whitehaven. Many different ships owned by the Midland Railway called at Douglas that summer, mainly on the Heysham service but some also to Barrow. Llandudno services were provided by three ships of the Liverpool & North Wales SSCo and two Blackpool-based steamers also visited the Island regularly. The other year-round service - which continued until 1943 - albeit under different ownership - was the Dublin & Silloth SS Co.'s service operated by the *Yarrow* (re-named *Assaroe* in 1929 when the service was taken over by Palgrave Murphy) which carried both passengers and cattle.

## World War One

The Midland Railway's pattern of services was interrupted by the outbreak of the First World War in 1914. The *Antrim, Donegal* and *Londonderry* were quickly requisitioned leaving the *Duchess of Devonshire* to provide a skeleton service on the Belfast route during the opening months of the war - before she herself was also requisitioned leading to the suspension of Belfast sailings. The *Manxman* was purchased by the Admiralty and converted into a seaplane carrier, being commissioned as H.M.S. *Manxman* in

December 1916. Even the *Wyvern* was taken and served throughout the war at Scapa Flow. The only war casualty from the Midland's Heysham fleet was the *Donegal* which was sunk by a German submarine in the English Channel in 1917 whilst serving as a hospital ship.

Laird Line appear to have been more successful in keeping their Heysham services operating during the First World War – perhaps because many of their vessels were already of some antiquity, like the *Dunure* of 1878 and the *Shamrock* of 1879. However the 1914-built *Maple* was on the Heysham – Dublin route for a time during the winter of 1915–16. The *Brier* had a major fire in Heysham on 15th December 1917 which was tackled by her crew. The local fire brigade insisted that the ship had her aft hold flooded to prevent ignition of inflammable cargo, as a result of which the ship sank. She was refloated and returned to service, surviving until 1933. On 22nd April 1918, the *Fern*, two hours into her passage from Dublin to Heysham was struck by a torpedo and sank within five minutes. She had 22 crew and 15 passengers on board but all except her gunner and cabin boy managed to get into her lifeboats and were saved.

## BETWEEN THE WARS

### Re-organisation and change

Regular passenger services from Heysham to Belfast and the Isle of Man did not resume until summer 1920. The year 1923 saw the re-organisation of the British railway companies into four major groupings. The new LMS (London Midland & Scottish Railway) brought the Midland under the same ownership as its rival L&NWR

(London & North Western Railway) who
operated shipping services from
Fleetwood jointly with the Lancashire
and Yorkshire Railway (L&Y). As a result
the Heysham and Fleetwood fleets were
merged and Heysham - Belfast services
were provided by the former L&NWR
vessels, the *Curraghmore* and the *Duke of
Argyll, Duke of Connaught* and *Duke of
Cumberland*. There was some interchange
of ships between Holyhead, Heysham and
Fleetwood in this period but the main
ships on the Manx route that year were
the *Menevia* (ex *Scotia*) from Holyhead
and the *Duke of Cornwall* although the
*Duchess of Devonshire* certainly made some
Douglas sailings as late as 1926.

In 1922 Laird Line had merged their operations with those of
G&J Burns to form Burns & Laird Lines and on 14th July 1926 their
Heysham - Dublin route was closed, the last sailing being taken by
the *Olive*. Their Londonderry service however continued until 1963.

The next change was the decision by the LMS to close its
Fleetwood operation and concentrate its Lancashire services on
Heysham. This became effective from 30th April 1928 and three new
and larger ships, built by Denny Bros. at Dumbarton, took over the
Heysham - Belfast route. These were the *Duke of Argyll*, the *Duke of
Lancaster* and the *Duke of Rothesay*. By now the *Londonderry* had been
transferred to the Tilbury - Dunkirk route and re-named the
*Flamand* and the *Antrim* was sold to the Isle of Man Steam Packet in

*The **Duke of York** was built for the LMS in 1935 as a slightly smaller version of the
1928 'Dukes' She had a fully glazed promenade deck and a higher forecastle than her
older half sisters. (John Hendy collection)*

1928 and became their *Ramsey Town*. With the closure of the
Fleetwood route, the "Ulster Express" from London Euston was
introduced to Heysham and the direct boat train from London, St
Pancras was withdrawn, although there were still through carriages
for Heysham on a Bradford express service. The "Ulster Express" ran
into Morecambe Promenade station where the mainline locomotive
was uncoupled and an 0-6-0 tank engine coupled to the other end
to take the train down to Heysham Harbour. There was also a

nightly train from Manchester Victoria where a large and permanent sign suspended over the platform read:

> **NORTH OF IRELAND**
> **(VIA) HEYSHAM**
> **BOAT TRAIN LEAVES THIS STATION**
> **EACH WEEKDAY 9.5 P.M.**
> **SUNDAYS 9.15 P.M.**
> **LUXURIOUS AND UP TO DATE FLEET OF**
> **STEAMERS**
> **DUKE OF ARGYLL**
> **DUKE OF LANCASTER**
> **DUKE OF ROTHESAY**

Having decided to concentrate their Lancashire shipping services at Heysham, not only did the LMS put new ships on the Belfast route, but they also modernised the harbour and its equipment between 1928 and 1936. The most obvious evidence of this period is the LMS Harbour Office block, built at the seaward end of the South Quay and standing disused in 2004. Between 1937 and 1940 the lower part of the wooden landings on the South Quay were replaced by reinforced concrete.

In November 1931 a major fire broke out on the *Duke of Lancaster* and she sank at her berth on the South Quay. After a difficult salvage operation she was repaired and returned to service in June 1932. After seasonal service from 1926 onwards, the *Curraghmore*, which had been built for the L&NWR Holyhead - Greenore service, was permanently transferred to Heysham in 1930 and renamed *Duke of Abercorn*. In June 1935 she was replaced by a

Harland and Wolff new build, the *Duke of York*. The new 'Duke' acted as fourth passenger ship at weekends but also assisted the *Slieve Bearnagh* - another turbine steamer from Denny Bros. - which arrived in 1936 to handle livestock and cargo shipments. She could carry 735 cattle and 291 horses. The *Princess Margaret* joined the Heysham fleet from Stranraer on a temporary basis in 1939.

## Manx services

The Midland Railway declined to re-purchase the *Manxman* from the Admiralty as the ship required too much re-furbishment after her war service (although she was later purchased by the IOM Steam Packet Company - and mainly used on their Liverpool service). There were no Isle of Man services from Heysham in 1919 but for

*The **Victoria** which inaugurated the Steam Packet's Heysham service on 23rd June 1928. (Author's collection)*

*The LMS owned **Menevia** (built as the **Scotia** for the London and North Western Railway in 1902) was placed on the Heysham – Isle of Man service in 1923. She worked the last LMS sailing on the route on 12th September 1927 and was scrapped the following year. She is seen here approaching Douglas. (John Hendy collection)*

*The **Duke of Abercorn** had been built as the **Curraghmore** for the LMS in 1919. When transferred permanently to Heysham in 1930 she was re-named. She was withdrawn in 1935 when the **Duke of York** replaced her. (John Hendy collection)*

1920 – 1922 the Manx services were in the hands of the *Duchess of Devonshire* and the 1893-built *City of Belfast* (both ex Barrow SNCo).

As part of the changes in 1928, the LMS had decided not to continue running the seasonal service to the Isle of Man and asked the Steam Packet to provide the service instead. The last LMS sailing from Heysham to Douglas was by the *Menevia* on 12th September 1927. As a railway company the LMS wanted the service to continue so that they could still bring the passengers to the port on their trains. A major concern for the Steam Packet was how to deal

with the extra traffic, particularly at peak weekends when, unlike the railway company, they did not have any "night" boats which could be called in to provide extra day sailings. At one stage in the negotiations, the Steam Packet offered to run the service during the week, leaving it to the Midland Railway to provide the weekend service.

Amongst the terms of the 7 year agreement there were requirements for the Steam Packet to:

● Provide satisfactory services … every weekday during the season, such services to be at least equal to those previously run by the LMS. [By 1931, the Steam Packet wanted to reduce the Isle of Man service to weekends only, "due to unsatisfactory returns", but the LMS would not agree to this and the service was maintained as per the agreement].

● To carry all traffic offering via Fleetwood or Heysham and that the arrangements which previously applied via Fleetwood limiting the number of passengers travelling by that route be cancelled. The bookings via Fleetwood and Heysham to be so regulated as to obviate as far as possible an overflow of passengers for any advertised service.

● The final deal included the sale of the *Antrim* for £7,500 and the *Duke of Cornwall* for £5,500. It had been resolved to call them *Ramsey* and *Rushen Castle* respectively but the register of shipping would not accept the former name so she became the *Ramsey Town*. There was also an arrangement whereby the LMS would provide a boat (if required) on up to five Saturdays in July/August each year. Under these arrangements the *Duke of Connaught* visited Douglas three times in August 1928 and the *Curraghmore* made three visits to the Island the following summer. In each case the charter rate was £150 per day, plus coal and port charges. The *Menevia* was also offered to the Steam Packet at scrap value but this offer was not taken up. When the 1928 season started the LMS provided free of charge one of their Masters who was about to retire, Captain Hunter, as Heysham pilot for the Steam Packet vessels between 23rd - 30th June. He was then employed directly by the Steam Packet for the month of July and paid £11/11/0 (£11.55) per week - after which his services were no longer required.

Despite having bought the two railway ships and had them refitted by Vickers at Barrow, it was a third - the *Victoria* built for the South Eastern & Chatham Railway - which the Steam Packet used to inaugurate their new route on 23rd June 1928. Having bought the *Victoria* with the Heysham route in mind, it was perhaps surprising that the *Snaefell* soon appeared on the route more frequently, although with a large fleet to from which to choose, several of the IOMSPCo vessels appeared in the port from time to time.

## Douglas Harbour Improvements

The intervention of the First World War had prevented further progress on harbour improvements in Douglas. When the subject was re-visited between 1921 – 1924 there again were arguments over whether more shelter from South Easterly gales should be given priority over providing more berths. In 1921 T B Hunter, Senior Superintendent Civil Engineer at the Admiralty was asked to advise and in his report the following July "preferred a scheme of outer works to be the most satisfactory solution" – but in view of the cost (over £1 million) recommended the extension of the Red Pier instead. The report was debated in Tynwald in January 1923 - but not adopted.

In 1923/4 proposals were drawn up for extending the Battery Pier by 153 metres - with the possibility of further extension later. Whereas this work would have given better protection to the existing harbour it did nothing to overcome the shortage of berths. Despite the approval of " all concerned in the trade of this port" the £750,000 scheme was abandoned owing to the great cost.

In 1928 the Lieutenant Governor instructed the Harbour Commissioners to look again at the situation. The Red Pier extension scheme was re-visited and what emerged was very much along the lines of the 1904 and 1908 proposals.

*Douglas Harbour in the early 1930s during the construction of the King Edward VIII Pier. The **Lady of Mann** (1) and **Ben-my-Chree** (4) lie at the outer end of the Victoria Pier with the **Snaefell** (4) closer to the town. (Photo courtesy of Manx National Heritage)*

## The scheme involved:

● Removal of the head of the Red Pier and its lighthouse

● Rebuilding 40 metres of the quay wall on the south side of the existing pier

● Removing the outer end of the Fort Anne jetty

● Deepening the harbour to give 4.6 metres of water at Low Water Spring Tides for 46 metres either side of the extension

● Constructing a masonry pier 140 metres long by 21 metres wide with its south side in line with the Red Pier.

● Constructing a submerged retaining wall across the river (inner harbour entrance) on the western dredging limit

● Constructing a viaduct 15 metres wide along the north side of the present pier and across the beach to the route of the Victoria Pier.

This time the work was put in hand at an estimated cost of £262,000 plus the cost of a small piece of land to be purchased from Steam Packet Company. Work was expected to take 6/7 years. The Western Viaduct was completed in June 1934 and the pier opened as the King Edward VIII Pier in 1936. It provided three more all-tide berths, one on the south and two on the north side. When the work was complete J C Brown, the Harbour Engineer, was able to write "Although there may remain much to be desired in the nature of sea works to create the ideal harbour, the piers and quays which exist constitute the most valuable tract of land in the Isle of Man, and Douglas Harbour - a prosaic thing to the casual observer - may justly claim to be the pulsating heart of the life of our little nation". In the case put forward to justify the expenditure the Harbour Commissioners had reported that they had been assured "by those fully competent to know" that the berth on the south side of the new pier "will be so sheltered in all states of the weather that there will be no necessity for steamers to go to Peel". Although more sheltered berthing was now available the harbour entrance was still open to NE gales and it was to be

nearly 50 years before that which was "to be desired in the nature of sea works to create the ideal harbour" came about.

## WORLD WAR TWO

### Heysham Port changes

Much change took place in Heysham port during the war years. The Trimpell refinery which came fully on-stream in July 1941 was built to produce aviation spirit - particularly for fighter aircraft. The main gasoil feedstock was brought from North or Central America by tankers which were too large to enter the port. It was therefore necessary to provide a deep-water berth outside the harbour. Initially

The *Snaefell*, *Duke of Rothesay*, *Duke of York*, *Duke of Lancaster* and *Princess Margaret* photographed by G Fairbank at Heysham on 4th August 1939. (Courtesy of Lancaster City Museums)

two mooring dolphins were erected about half a mile NE of the harbour entrance and then a reinforced concrete approach pier was built to carry the pipeline to the refinery. The first tanker to berth at the new facility was the *Laurent Meeus* on 24th October 1941 – although feedstock had been brought in earlier that year by tankers mooring off and using an underwater pipeline. The berthing of tankers provided new work for the *Wyvern* which remained at Heysham through the war.

## The Belfast ships go to war

The Heysham LMS steamers were all requisitioned immediately on the outbreak of war:

The *Duke of Argyll* was in Southampton by 8th September 1939 and remained on trooping duties in the Channel until transferred to the Clyde at the end of June 1940. She was released from government service the following November and returned to the Belfast – Heysham route until requisitioned again on 1st May 1942. She was then fitted out as an infantry landing ship, taking part in the Normandy landings in June 1944, after which she was fitted out on the Clyde as a hospital carrier. She remained in that service until 25th June 1945 and on 5th August sailed from Southampton to Belfast for refit.

The *Duke of Lancaster*'s first war mission was to take naval ratings to Douglas on 4th September 1939 after which she sailed from Avonmouth and Cardiff until she returned to service at Heysham mid October. She was not requisitioned again until January 1944 when she went to Glasgow for conversion to a hospital carrier. In this capacity she served at the Normandy landings and remained on the south coast until released for refit on the Clyde, returning to

*The Ocean Jetty was opened outside Heysham Harbour in 1941 to provide a deep water tanker berth, but this was demolished in 1976, although rarely used after 1967 following the building of a pipeline from Tranmere.*

civilian duties in December 1945.

After reaching Southampton on 10th September 1939 the *Duke of Rothesay* made two sailings to France before moving to the Bristol Channel – but was back in Heysham mid October. It would appear that the LMS were particularly keen to get her back and had offered the Holyhead-based *Scotia* to replace her. The 'Rothesay' remained on the Belfast service until going to the Mersey for conversion to an Infantry Landing Ship in September 1943, at which point her place at Heysham was taken by another Holyhead ship, the *Cambria*. The 'Duke' was converted to a Hospital Carrier in time for the Normandy landings and continued in this role until March 1945 when engine problems necessitated a refit from which she emerged as a troop carrier. She served in this role on the Harwich – Hook route until 1947.

The *Duke of York's* first war sailing was from Southampton on 20th September, although she had arrived at Avonmouth on the 8th. She was involved both in the transport of the British Expeditionary Force to Cherbourg and Le Havre and subsequently the evacuation of British troops from NW France. She was back at Heysham by the beginning of July 1940 and remained on the Belfast route until the end of April 1942. She was then converted into an Infantry Landing Ship and commissioned as HMS *Duke of Wellington* at the end of May. In this capacity she served both in the Dieppe Raid and later the Normandy Landings. She paid off as a warship in February 1945, resumed her previous name, and then operated as a troopship first

*Dredging has always been required at Heysham, particularly around the harbour entrance. The Larne-built **Rossall** of 1921 was owned by British Railways when this photo was taken in May 1955. (Ian Harmsworth)*

from Tilbury to Ostend and later on the Harwich – Hook service until released in mid-November 1946.

## Other ships and services

The LNER-owned *Dewsbury* made a brief appearance in the autumn of 1939. Between July 1941 and August 1943 the *Irwell* ran on the Heysham – Belfast service. She was an LMS-owned cargo ship which had previously been based in Goole. The Southern Railway's cargo ship *Deal* was used on the route in 1945 between 22nd April and 1st August. The *Louth,* owned by B&I, also made some wartime appearances on charter.

The Burns and Laird service to Londonderry, usually run by the 1936-built *Lairdsbank*, stopped carrying passengers during the war

*In 1936 the **Slieve Bearnagh** was the first cargo vessel built for the Heysham-Belfast service. She was scrapped in 1972. (Ian Harmsworth)*

*The 1934 built **Princess Maud** at Heysham in April 1965. She was sold to Greek owners for further service later that summer. (Ian Harmsworth)*

*The 1928-built **Duke of Argyll** at Heysham in 1955 – her final year of service. (Ian Harmsworth)*

but continued as a cargo only service until 1963. Between 1941 and 1943 there was also a twice weekly service from Heysham to Greenore. With the coming of war Manx ferry services to Heysham again stopped, with the *Victoria* returning light ship back to Douglas after the cancellation of her scheduled sailing on 4th September 1939. She remained on the Steam Packet's limited wartime service to Liverpool [Fleetwood from 1941] until taken up for Combined Operations duties in April 1942. The only Steam Packet vessel positively identified as sailing from Heysham on war service was the *Lady of Mann* whilst on troop transport duties in December 1940 and January 1941, although she may also have made calls between May 1942 and July 1943.

**1945-1980**

At the end of the Second World War it could be argued that Heysham Harbour at last stood on the threshold of the growth that its originators had envisaged nearly half a century earlier, but which had never come. The war had brought new industry to the area and the port now had an oil jetty capable of handling ocean going tankers. The LMS Irish Sea fleet, unlike that of the Isle of Man Steam Packet, had come through the war without loss and all the ships duly returned to service on the Heysham – Belfast route.

Shell had taken over the Trimpel Refinery near the port and in 1947 had already installed an additional oil berth for bunkering ships alongside the North Quay using a pontoon which had been part of the Mulberry Harbours used in the 1944 Normandy landings – but this was removed in March 1977. Tankers up to 25,000 tons were able to use the oil jetty and Shell took two tugs on charter from

The **Mona's Isle** leaving Heysham on 15th July 1953 – the first scheduled sailing to the Isle of Man since 1939. (Courtesy of Lancaster City Museums)

CHAPTER 2

A Century of Operations

*The **Duke of Argyll** just after her launch at Harland & Wolff on 12th January 1956. After leaving the Irish Sea in 1975 she was burned out in Hong Kong in 1995. (Heysham Port)*

*The **Duke of Rothesay** at Donegall Quay. (Ian Collard)*

*Container handling at Heysham's North Quay. (Heysham Port)*

James Fisher - the *Fishershill* and the *Fisherstown* This relegated the harbour's own *Wyvern* to third tug for tanker berthing, but these duties were inevitably tidal, so preventing the *Wyvern* resuming her summer passenger sailings to Fleetwood. However the size of tanker being used was soon too big for Heysham and in October 1967 a 70 mile pipeline from Tranmere was opened, after which there was no further need for feedstock to be brought in by sea. The Ocean Jetty was demolished in 1976 and the following year the refinery itself was closed down, although the tank farm and associated rail facilities remained operational until 1983.

ICI, who had also been involved in the wartime developments, continued to make nitro-chalk and from 1950 also produced nitric acid at their Heysham plant. In 1965 they installed a pipeline from their works to the coaster berth on the North Quay for the purpose of loading liquefied anhydrous ammonia which was shipped to Glasgow, Belfast and Arklow using the *Quentin* - owned by G Gibson & Co of Leith. This operation was closed by 1985.

By the end of 1980 nearly all the post-war hopes for Heysham port seemed to have been extinguished. All the Sealink Belfast services had closed - the future was looking bleak for Heysham port and its staff. All that was left was the general cargo operations which James Fisher had established on the South Quay in 1972 and a one ship Sealink-Manx Line ro-ro operation to the Isle of Man. There was not much life, but there was still some hope.

The **Duke of Lancaster** during her early career on the Irish Sea. (Ian Collard collection)

## Belfast services return to normal

After the war all four railway ships went to Belfast for extensive refits. The *Duke of Lancaster* returned to service on 12th December 1945 and the 'Argyll' was back on 11th February 1946. The 'Rothesay' and the 'York' were retained on the Harwich – Hook trooping service and did not resume commercial operation until the summer and autumn of 1947 respectively. The *Duke of York* was transferred to Harwich at the beginning of 1949 and was replaced at Heysham by the cargo-only *Slieve Bloom* transferred from Holyhead to run alongside the *Slieve Bearnagh*, but the next year she was

*When the three 'Dukes' were introduced in 1956 only two were required to run the basic mid-week service. This enabled the **Duke of Lancaster** to be used for 12 day cruises in the early 1960s, but, as in this picture, the spare ship would usually lay over in Heysham. (John Hendy collection)*

exchanged for the *Slieve Bawn*. The Irish passenger trade recovered well and extra capacity was provided by the *Princess Maud* and also by the introduction of day sailings. By 1955-6 trade had developed to the extent that British Railways – London Midland Region (for in 1948 all the railway companies had been nationalised) introduced three larger (4450 ton) steamers - again using the names *Duke of Lancaster*, *Duke of Argyll* and *Duke of Rothesay*. These were built as pure passenger ships which carried 1,800 passengers, and in the early 1960s the *Duke of Lancaster* was used on 12-day cruises from Heysham to Scotland and northern European destinations as far

away as Norway. The pattern of boat trains remained with the "Ulster Express" from London Euston, the "Belfast Boat Express" from Manchester Victoria and a direct service from Leeds which, after 1966, ran via Carnforth. The "Belfast Boat Express" was to be the last British Rail steam-hauled named train in May 1968.

During 1958/59 and 1961/63 the Victoria Channel in Belfast was again widened and deepened, as well as being extended another 3.2 kilometres further to seaward. This now gave a channel with a width of 152 metres and a depth 9.1 metres below harbour datum, but of greater significance this work also included the provision of a 430 metre diameter turning circle opposite today's Victoria Terminals. Previous to this the mail steamers had usually had to go astern the full length of the Victoria Channel right up to Donegall Quay. In April 1960 the Pilot Light Vessel *Lady Dixon* was withdrawn. She had

*The **Duke of Argyll** at the Donegall Quay linkspan on 6th April 1975 – after completing her final journey from Heysham. (Paul Clegg)*

provided a base for the Belfast Pilots since July 1944 at the entrance to the channel up to Belfast. Thereafter the pilots used fast pilot cutters from a shore base at Carrickfergus.

## The start of containerisation

Between 1957 and 1962 three new container berths were built at Belfast on the west side of the Herdman Channel and two existing berths at Spencer Dock and Ballast Quay were converted for container handling. In 1958 British Railways introduced two container ships on the Heysham – Belfast route: the *Container Enterprise* and the *Container Venturer*. These carried "railway containers" and ran from a new container berth on the North Quay at Heysham. Initially a 13-ton capacity crane was provided but from early 1971 a 30-ton portal crane was installed. These ships replaced the container service which had been operated from Fleetwood on behalf of BR by James Fisher to Belfast and Larne. By 1969 the *Selby* and the chartered *Derwent Fisher* had joined the operation and each of the 'Container' vessels ran in tandem with one of them on the 6 night a week service. By now the ISO container had arrived and the service was carrying ISO containers 5 nights a week with the sixth sailing reserved for

The **Duke of Lancaster** *arriving at Donegall Quay. The normal practice, due to the width of the River Lagan, was for the vessels to swing in Belfast Lough and make their approach astern. (Ian Collard)*

"conventional" containers. In 1971 the Belfast terminal had moved to Gotto Wharf.

## The arrival of ro-ro

The first ro-ro (roll-on roll-off) berth was provided in Belfast as early as 1950 at Pollock Basin East for the Transport Ferry Service which ran from Preston. [This was replaced in 1968 by a berth on

45

the Herdman Channel] The next ro-ro berths to be completed were at Donegall Quay in 1967 for the Belfast Steamship Liverpool service and for Burns & Laird Lines' Ardrossan service. The ro-ro berth for the Heysham service was built at the same quay between 1969 and 1970 and this included a new two storey terminal building with access to the ships by covered passenger gangway from the upper floor.

Traffic patterns were changing, with more and more passengers wanting to take their cars with them. The *Duke of Rothesay* had been converted to a side loading car ferry and transferred to service at Fishguard in 1967. Although boat trains were still provided to Heysham for the main sailings from London, Manchester and Leeds, local rail services had been axed. The *Duke of Argyll* and the *Duke of Lancaster* were converted to stern loading car ferries early in 1970 at Harland and Wolff in Belfast after which they had a capacity for 1,200 passengers and up to 105 cars. They also carried 'Brutes'

*The **Container Enterprise** leaving Heysham for the last time on 16th December 1978 following closure of the Belfast lo-lo container service.(Ian Harmsworth)*

(British Rail Universal Trolley Equipment) on the car deck – caged trolleys mainly for the carriage of mail and parcels, but also newspapers. If 300 Brutes were carried car capacity would be reduced to 35 cars. There was minimal space available for caravans or high headroom vehicles.

To handle this new traffic a 76 metre long linkspan was built in the SE corner of Heysham harbour, with a new railway station and passenger terminal alongside it. This opened on 22nd May 1970 - when the new two-ship car ferry service was inaugurated. Sailings were 6 nights a week with departures at 23.45 ex Heysham and 22.30 from Belfast. The service increased to 7 nights a week in July/August and daylight sailings also operated at peak periods. Crossing time was 7 hrs 5 mins. The total investment in the new service including terminal facilities and the conversion and

*The **Hibernia** ran from Heysham to Dun Laoghaire whilst the rail access to Holyhead was severed. (Heysham Port)*

upgrading of the two ships was around £2 million.

The response to this new service was considerably below British Rail's expectations and by July 1970 - only weeks after the service opened - they wrote to the Steam Packet advising that for summer 1971they were considering routing their day services via Douglas. The plan was inevitably and vigorously opposed by the Steam Packet board and was withdrawn within a matter of weeks "for various reasons" - of which one might have been the absence of a linkspan in Douglas Harbour.

At this time there were also Irish cargo and cattle sailings from middle of the South Quay (berth 3) at Heysham. Livestock was carried on the *Slieve Bearnagh* ex Belfast on Tuesdays / Thursdays and occasionally on Saturday nights. The matching sailings were provided by the chartered *Firth Fisher* which did not carry livestock. Lairage was still provided in the port - for up to 853 "fat cattle" - and the

*The **Penda**, seen here at Heysham on 18th March 1978, was on the Sealink Belfast – Heysham service. (Ian Harmsworth)*

adjacent cattle dock would hold up to 34 wagons. Extra cargo sailings were arranged when required using a variety of ships. The introduction of ro-ro ships on various routes was soon to spell the end of "conventional" cargo and cattle boats with the final shipments from Northern Ireland being made in December 1971 and a last sailing from Dublin by the B&I ship *Meath* arriving on 1st January 1972.

## Heysham – Dun Laoghaire

Two new larger container ships the *Brian Boroime* and the *Rhodri Mawr* were due for delivery in November/December 1970. The plan was that these would replace the four ships at Heysham but that the service would then operate from Holyhead. This plan was thwarted when the railway line to Holyhead was closed at the end of May 1970 as a result of fire damage to the Britannia Bridge across the

*Sealink's ro-ro **Dalriada** leaving Heysham on 30th March 1979. (Ian Harmsworth)*

*The **Lune Bridge** at Heysham in February 1980.(Ian Harmsworth)*

*This 1971 view of Heysham Harbour shows the old railway station to the left and the new one to the right. (Peter Joslin)*

*The **Lune Bridge** and **Lagan Bridge** were the final vessels on the Sealink ro-ro service from Heysham to Belfast. They only worked on the route in 1980.(Ian Harmsworth)*

*The new railway station, terminal and linkspan under construction – photographed by Peter Sunderland in March 1970. (Courtesy of Lancaster City Museums)*

Menai Straits. The outcome was that the two ships operated on the Belfast - Heysham route until the end of January 1972 - but container operations at Heysham continued until the end of 1978. - The consequences of the Holyhead rail link being severed was an increase in traffic and services at Heysham which was to last for 20 months. The Holyhead - Dun Laoghaire mail ships *Cambria* and *Hibernia* sailed nightly from Heysham, with connecting boat trains from London Euston. They operated from the western end of the South Quay, not requiring use of the linkspan, and such few cars as they carried were craned on and off. The former Fishguard and Rosslare steamer *St David* also made some appearances on this service in 1970. Road access to Holyhead was still available so the car ferries still ran from there each night but in the peak summer season on Tuesdays, Thursdays and Saturdays the car ferry laying over for the day in Dun Laoghaire (the *Holyhead Ferry I* or the *Dover)* ran a day sailing to Heysham, arriving at 14.50 and returning an hour later. Connecting train services to and from Leeds were provided in connection with these sailings. Once Holyhead fully re-opened there was an inevitable diversion of traffic back to that route.

## Decline sets in

The Belfast passenger traffic also went into steep decline following the civil unrest in Northern Ireland to the extent that in April 1975 passenger and car ferry services to Belfast were closed and 400 seafarers were made redundant. The final boat trains ran into Heysham on 5th April 1975 and departed after the arrival of the steamer early the next morning. The Belfast-Ardrossan passenger service closed the following year.

By summer 1975 Heysham had no passenger, car ferry services or trains using the station, terminal and linkspan which had only been completed five years earlier. The cattle trade had gone, the refinery was soon to close… and a nuclear power station was being built on the land originally intended for the building of the enclosed dock. The Burns & Laird service on the Heysham-Londonderry route had closed in 1963 – with the final sailing worked by the *Lairdsbank* Did the port have any future?

The container service struggled on and later in 1975 the first ro-ro freight ship, the *Penda*, was put on the Belfast route by Sealink in a joint venture with Belfast Steamship Services to carry lorries and trailers. This ship was to run out of Heysham for three different operators over the next 20 years and is best remembered as the Isle of Man Steam Packet's *Peveril* . This service ran to ro-ro berths recently constructed at York Dock in Belfast. When the container service closed in 1978 the *Penda* was joined by the *Dalriada* but in 1980 both ships were replaced by the larger sisters *Lagan Bridge* and *Lune Bridge* which operated 6 nights a week, plus 3 daylight sailings. Unfortunately this service incurred heavy losses and closed on 13th December 1980. At the same time Containerway and Roadferry had given notice that they were to transfer their Lift on/Lift off service from Heysham to Garston in 1981. This service had operated from Preston until 1975.

## Steam Packet services return to Heysham in 1953 …. but only until 1974

The Isle of Man Steam Packet showed no alacrity in returning to Heysham and their first scheduled post-war sailing was not until 1953, although the *Mona's Isle* had operated a charter two years earlier. The service only re-started after an approach from Mr J Gaunt, who had been their pre-war Morecambe agent, supported by the Town Clerks of Morecambe and Lancaster. It was seen primarily as a day excursion opportunity for holidaymakers in Morecambe rather than a means of transporting people to the Island for their holidays. Seven (Wednesday) sailings were offered in 1953, but as they showed a profit of £2,414 on takings of £6,627, the Steam Packet decided to offer 8 (Thursday) sailings the following year - Mr Gaunt having advised that there were fewer conflicting attractions on Thursdays. No connecting boat trains were provided but as the Steam Packet were providing a daily summer service from Fleetwood, the Heysham service was only seen as trying to tap the local market.

## Improvements in Douglas

In Douglas the Victoria Pier was widened by 5.8 metres along its seaward side, work being completed in 1953. This was required as more vehicular traffic was being handled, much of it craned on and off the conventional ferries - unless the tide happened to be at the appropriate level. Even double-decked buses for use on the Island were carried on the foredeck of the passenger steamers, but due to the absence of large enough cranes they had to wait until the deck was level with the quay before they could be driven off. There was also an increase in parcels and mail traffic which was handled on the passenger steamers - which led to more vehicles needing to come onto the pier.

In November 1957 Douglas Town Council held a meeting with the Steam Packet to discuss a number of complaints - including arrangements for the carrying of cars and motor cycles – which they

*This photograph taken by Peter Joslin during the construction of the Heysham Nuclear Power station in June 1971 shows the **Slieve Donard** and either the **Cambria** or **Hibernia** which were operating to Dun Laoghaire during the closure of the Britannia railway bridge across the Menai Straits. The "Belfast Shed" and the original railway station can be seen beyond the ships.*

felt to be quite unsatisfactory. Nothing further happened until in December 1959 a report was presented to the Steam Packet Board which referred to "possible intervention by other companies interested in the car-ferry business" if they did not take action. No names were mentioned but the board agreed in principle to look at a car ferry capable of carrying 1,400 passengers and 60/70 cars.

As there was no linkspan in Douglas Harbour - and the perceived wisdom at the time was that the shelter in the harbour was inadequate for one to be safely built – a system for the loading and discharging of cars at all states of the tide had to be devised. A draft specification of the ship was drawn up and seven yards invited to come up with quotations and design proposals by 30th April 1960. Most of the designs submitted required vehicle lifts to some or all decks and some required cut away hulls to handle them, but Cammell Laird came up with an on-board ramp system which could be used at all states of the tide and it was on that basis that they were awarded the order to build the *Manx Maid* which entered service in 1962. The Steam Packet was to build three further car ferries using this principle – the *Ben-my-Chree* (1966), *Mona's Queen* (1972) and *Lady of Mann* (1976).

In 1960 construction work started on the new Sea Terminal buildings in Douglas which were completed in 1967, providing an extensive waiting area, as well as offices and a restaurant.

In 1969 Norwest Hovercraft, who at the time were operating a short lived service from Fleetwood using the *Stella Marina,* approached the IOM Harbour Board for provision of a "stern-loading linkspan" in Douglas, to be built at their own expense and for their own exclusive use. This never happened and the service closed the following year as the replacement vessel *Norwest Laird* (ex *Lochiel*) proved quite unsatisfactory.

In 1972 the Isle of Man Harbour Board had Douglas Harbour surveyed by the National Ports Council who, as a result of wave tests, recommended a 247 metre extension to the Battery Pier - which was supposed to reduce wave heights by 89% - and the building of a linkspan for ro-ro vessels. This led to a scheme being produced in 1975 not only to build the current extended breakwater and install a linkspan on the Victoria Pier, but also to build a second linkspan parallel to the first alongside a new pier to be built between the Edward and Victoria Piers. This would have rendered the two berths on the north side of the Edward Pier inaccessible, as there would have been a cross berth built between the heads of the two piers. It was reported at the time that the linkspan proposals were regarded as unwarranted interference in the running of the Steam Packet.

Heysham services to and from the Isle of Man had remained at a low ebb - never progressing beyond one or two sailings a week and only in July and August. These services finished at the end of the 1974 season with the *Mona's Isle*, the first Steam Packet ship to visit Heysham after the Second World War, taking the final sailing from Douglas on 28th August 1974. That year the service ran at a loss - 5,636 passengers travelled to the Isle of Man - down from 8,489 the previous year and as fuel costs had risen 300% in 12 months the company could see no hope of returning the route to profitability.

## Manx Line

Towards the end of 1977 the Isle of Man Government, who at the time were the largest single shareholder in the Steam Packet with a 13.6% holding, asked to be allowed to appoint a director to the Company's board and, at virtually the same time, announced plans to spend £650,000 to finance part of the facilities for the establishment of a rival operator. Not only were the IOM Government told there was no vacancy on the Steam Packet Board, they were subjected to a blistering attack from Major T E Brownsdon, the Steam Packet chairman. He was particularly incensed that "an unknown company" was to get the exclusive use of a berth in Douglas Harbour when they had only put up half the money. He did however concede that if they had paid for the total installation – or it had been provided by the Harbour Board for the use of all operators, then he could not have raised any "reasonable objection". He listed many more objections to the scheme – including the prophetic one that, exposed to easterly winds, the "installation would be at great risk of damage". Nevertheless he told his shareholders in February 1978 "the evidence available to us does not indicate that ro-ro would provide better or cheaper services to the Isle of Man".

The "unknown company" was Manx Line and the arrangement they had come to was that the approach viaduct to their linkspan on Victoria Pier would be financed by the IOM Government whereas they would finance the actual linkspan themselves. By the time Major Brownsdon had addressed his shareholders, Taylor Woodrow had already been at work in Douglas Harbour for two months building the approach viaduct for the new linkspan, and only the previous day Geoff Duke had held a press conference in London to announce the new service to Heysham. This was

*The **Monte Castillo** arrives at Heysham for berthing trials on 23rd March 1978. After a major refit she entered service for Manx Line as the **Manx Viking**. (Photo: The Visitor Newspaper Courtesy of Lancaster City Museums)*

to use the two year old *Monte Castillo* which had been built for Aznar Line's UK-Canaries route. She duly appeared at both Douglas and Heysham for berthing trials on 23rd March 1978 before going for an extensive refit, which included the fitting of a bow door, at Leith. Duke's partner was Edmundson-Ronagency who had their own unit load operation in opposition to the Steam Packet, which

they proposed to divert to the new Manx Line.

After many delays the new service started on 26th August 1978 – but two weeks later had to be withdrawn when the *Manx Viking* suffered severe engine damage. In cash flow terms this was catastrophic and, had it not been for the intervention of James Fisher and the assistance of Sealink, Manx Line could not have survived.

Alternative arrangements for freight were made with a number of charters until the *Manx Viking* returned, but on 1st December 1978 yet another catastrophe arose when the new linkspan was severely damaged during an easterly storm. As had happened with previous developments, the decision was taken to take the risk of installing the linkspan without improving the shelter in the harbour - although the need to do this had been clearly recognised. Manx Line maintained a lift on – lift off freight only service through the winter, using chartered coasters including the *Eden Fisher* and the *Poole Fisher*. In May 1979 the *Manx Viking* returned from an extensive refit in Belfast and used a temporary linkspan on the north side of the Edward Pier until repairs to the Victoria Pier linkspan were completed in July. With the resources of Sealink behind it a number of charter vessels were brought in to maintain services whilst the *Manx Viking* underwent refit. The *Viking III* and *Antrim Princess* both covered in 1980

*The **Manx Viking** in her original Manx Line colours. (Ian Harmsworth)*

## The Steam Packet reacts

Despite the scorn which the Steam Packet had heaped on the Manx Line operation, they engaged the services of Burness, Corlett and Partners to advise whether there was anywhere in Douglas Harbour where a ro-ro berth could be constructed. They reported in April 1979 and, after consultations with the IOM Harbour Board, the Steam Packet were given temporary permission to site a linkspan on the south side of the King Edward Pier – the anticipation being that it would be moved to the north side on completion of a new breakwater. Before the Steam Packet ordered their own linkspan, discussions were held with Sealink with a view to sharing the existing facility "after it had been modified to make it safer, particularly in bad weather" but the terms offered would have required the Steam Packet to charter a Sealink-manned vessel and close down their own cargo operations and make their Manx crews redundant.

In November 1979 Tynwald had approved the expenditure of £7.2 million for the extension of the Battery Pier to at last provide the required "tranquillisation of the harbour" and within twelve months the Steam Packet ordered their own linkspan from the Finnish manufacturer OY Navire AB at a cost of £1.5 million. This was towed into Douglas on 2nd June 1981 by the tug *Skua* and positioned on the south side of the King Edward Pier. The *NF Jaguar* – which had seen previous service for Sealink from Heysham as the *Penda* – was chartered from P&O to operate a freight only service to Liverpool and this was inaugurated on 19th June 1981.

## 1980 –1989

In the early 1980s Heysham was described in one of the local newspapers as " a run-down Lancashire port". Sealink would happily have sold the port at this stage - but who would have wanted to buy it? The need to attract new and lasting business was well recognised by the local management as being essential if the port was to have any future. The prospects for reviving the Irish traffic appeared minimal - yet soon Martin Miller, at that time Northern Sector Manager for Sealink, was able to write "1983 does indeed look a great year for the Sealink port of Heysham".

Gas had been discovered under the Irish Sea and two developments took place which led to a change in the fortunes of the port. On 1st December 1981 the exploration drilling rig *Western Apollo II* was towed into Heysham Harbour for repairs to damage sustained on passage from Singapore. Although the repairs only took a matter of weeks its presence in the harbour was a very visible symbol of renewed activity in the port.

Although never used for its intended purpose, the Tarmac group established a sea dredged aggregate depot at the Fish Quay in 1981, but this closed again in the late 1980s following the completion of the Heysham II power station.

As a "railway" port, Heysham had originally been laid out on the basis that virtually all landside passenger and cargo traffic would move In and out by rail, so road access was minimal. Only with the building of the Nuclear Power station and the development of the gas field supply base was this problem addressed. For the nuclear power station to be built it was necessary to open up road access to the south side of the port and this led to the building in 1967 of the

*A Sea Cadet band helped the **Manx Viking** celebrate her 1000th crossing on 18th February 1980.*

bridge across the railway which is now used for access to the passenger and car ferry terminal, the South Quay berths and the power station itself.

The building of the gas field supply base similarly led to infrastructure improvements to the north side of the port without which the further development of the ro-ro freight business could not have happened. Freight access is via Port Way - to the east of which is a small industrial park built on the site of the old Shell refinery.

As ro-ro traffic grew, so general cargo operations in Heysham port declined. In 1989 conventional cargo through the Fisher Terminal peaked with 105 ships calling during the year. Much of the success of this terminal was due to labour difficulties in Liverpool and as these diminished it became more difficult to attract general cargo through Heysham.

## The return of Northern Ireland services

In 1983 Seabridge Marine of Oban attempted to start a Belfast – Heysham passenger, car and freight service but could not get a manning agreement from the National Union of Seamen who feared that jobs on existing Irish Sea services might be jeopardised.

In March 1984 Scruttons plc had set up a new subsidiary Belfast Freight Ferries [BFF] which started as a single-ship operation from Heysham using the chartered *Stena Sailor.* This service ran initially to Donegall Quay in Belfast. In April 1985 they replaced her with the *Peveril* which was chartered from the Steam Packet Company.

Belfast Freight Ferries had originally chartered their ships through Cenargo but, following some differences between them, Cenargo established their own ro-ro freight operation to Warrenpoint in 1985 under the name Merchant Ferries. In 1986 BFF chartered the *Spheroid* to replace the *Peveril and* also increased their service by putting the *Saga Moon* on as second ship.

## Isle of Man developments

The new Douglas breakwater, built by French Kier, was opened by Princess Alexandra in 1983. The core is of quarried rubble overlaid with stones weighing between 2.5 and 6 tonnes and the seaward side is protected by 4,000 concrete interlocking armour units, each weighing 23 tonnes and known as "stabits". Large tracked cranes were used in the work operating both from the shore and from floating pontoons as required. The building of the new breakwater required changes to the harbour approaches and a deeper channel had to be blasted through the end of the reef known as "The Flakes" which runs east from the Conister Rock (on which

the Tower of Refuge is built). Initially the Harbour Board attempted this work themselves but in the summer of 1981 a drilling barge was chartered from the Dutch company Royal Volker Stevin, who also supplied a bucket dredger for the project. Before these plans were finalised there was extensive consultation with the Harbourmaster and Shipmasters who requested a substantial dolphin be built at the seaward end of the new breakwater to prevent ships being swept onto the breakwater and damaged below the waterline.

In 1988, following completion of the breakwater, the old wooden cattle staging was removed from the Battery Pier, and a new tanker berth built in its place. The new hardstanding created on the seaward side of the Battery Pier provided space for pressurised gas

*The Princess Alexandra breakwater at Douglas was built behind, and extended beyond the Battery Pier as can be seen by this photograph taken midway through its construction. (Stan Basnett)*

*The tug* **Bramley Moore** *towing the Steam Packet Navire linkspan into Douglas Bay after repairs in November 1989. (Stan Basnett)*

tanks. At the time all gas used on the Island was imported by sea and all electricity was generated on Island from oil-fired power stations.

The tremendous amount of work being done in Douglas harbour in the late 1970s and early 1980s led to the establishment of the Laxey Towing Company in 1978. They provided tugs and workboats for use around the harbour and when work was at its peak in 1981 they had three tugs based in Douglas the *Cabot*, the *Union* and the *Salisbury*. In the following 25 years the Douglas-based company developed to provide towage, cranage, dredging, heavy haulage, and ship painting services and coastal cruises using the *Karina*. The company's owner is also the Douglas pilot and the Douglas pilot boat is often used to take Mersey pilots off deep-sea vessels in bad weather.

As the breakwater was being built, the Heysham route was at last

being operated reliably by the *Manx Viking* and with Sealink now backing the operation there was no difficulty in providing replacement vessels whenever needed to cover refits. The Steam Packet reduced its passenger fleet, relying increasingly on its side loading car ferries, and all its freight was carried on the *Peveril*, as the *NF Jaguar* had been renamed. Due to the high charter fees the operation of the *Peveril* was quite uneconomic so the vessel was then purchased in 1982 by James Fisher Ltd (who had, with Sealink, bailed out Manx Line four years earlier) and demise chartered to the Steam Packet. Whilst this helped the economics of the operation considerably it did nothing to deal with the deepening industrial relations problems facing the Liverpool freight service. Constant strikes led to major defections of freight customers to Manx Line and by July 1984 the Steam Packet were making a loss, only carrying half the freight. As they were unlikely to recover their share of the freight market they decided to combine their freight and passenger operations for 1985, purchasing the *Tamira* (ex *Free Enterprise III)* for the purpose, chartering out the *Peveril* and selling the two steam turbine car ferries *Manx Maid* and *Ben-my-Chree.* There was no announcement over where the "new" ship – re-named *Mona's Isle* - would run to, and none of the UK passenger berths the company used had linkspans.

## Sealink Manx Line

Although Sealink Manx Line was probably not making profits, it had certainly severely damaged the business of the Steam Packet, particularly on the freight side. After its difficult start the service became well established and whenever the *Manx Viking* needed a refit chartered tonnage was brought in to maintain the year round service, the *Ailsa Princess* being used during the winter of 1981/2 and the *Villandry* in 1983. In 1983 UK operators were, for the first time, allowed to take motor coaches to the Isle of Man and it was only Sealink Manx Line who were able to offer this facility

## Sea Containers take over

In July 1984 the British Government privatised its Sealink railway shipping operations and as a result of this move both the port of Heysham and Sealink-Manx Line came under the control of the Bermuda-based Sea Containers. Sea Containers then bought a 40% stake in the Steam Packet and from 1st April 1985 the two operations were merged, under the Steam Packet name with Heysham becoming the main UK port.

*The need for the breakwater at Douglas is well illustrated by the battering it was taking even during construction.(Stan Basnett)*

## The Steam Packet returns to Heysham

This new situation restored the Steam Packet monopoly in the Manx trade, but also meant that both Douglas Harbour linkspans were now under their control – a situation which was to cause some friction between the company and the Manx Government, and which had some bearing on the development of facilities in both Douglas and Heysham harbours in years to come. In the Isle of Man this was seen as "Sea Containers taking over the Steam Packet" but in Heysham it was seen as the "Steam Packet taking over Manx Line". The combined service planned to offer three sailings a day in each direction using the recently purchased *Mona's Isle* and the *Manx Viking*. The Steam Packet's Liverpool ro-ro freight service using the *Peveril* was discontinued, with that vessel being chartered out to

*The **Lady of Mann** arrives from Douglas in 1985. (Ian Collard)*

Belfast Freight Ferries, to replace the *Stena Sailor*. It was anticipated that all Isle of Man freight could be carried on the passenger vessels, despite neither ship having any open deck for carrying hazardous cargo.

The first day of April 1985 should have seen the start of the new improved thrice-daily service to Heysham operated by the *Manx Viking* and the *Mona's Isle*. Owing to an industrial dispute at Heysham (about the introduction of the *Peveril* on the Belfast route) the linkspan was blocked for passengers and their cars and the service was opened by the side loaders *Mona's Queen* and *Lady of Mann*. The new *Mona's Isle* arrived in Douglas on 3rd April only to find she would not fit onto either of the linkspans in the harbour without further modifications. By 19th April it was admitted that the *Mona's Isle* had serious dead weight and handling problems.

The newly merged company found itself with inadequate capacity for the 1985 TT races and ended up chartering back the *Ben-my-Chree* [V] which it had sold out of service at the end of the previous season. The 'Ben' ran out of Heysham, a port she had never previously visited, between 25th May and 10th June 1985. The new combined service carried 13.7% fewer passengers in summer 1985 than the separate Liverpool and Heysham services had done the previous year. Although the merger increased Steam Packet revenue by 25%, losses doubled in part due to the unsatisfactory performance of the *Mona's Isle*. By August it was decided to withdraw the ship and she made her final voyage on 5th October 1985 – only 6 months after entering Steam Packet service.

The next day she was replaced by the *Antrim Princess* which was crewed by the Steam Packet but chartered from Sealink. After re-fit she was re-named *Tynwald* but was never owned by the Steam

*Manx Viking.* (*John Hendy collection*)

Packet. The *Manx Viking* was bare-boat chartered to the Steam
Packet, her crew having transferred to the Steam Packet on
completion of the merger, so until she was withdrawn on 29th
September 1986 the Heysham route was in the hands of two ships
owned by Sea Containers. In the first year the combined operation
lost over £3 million – about half of which was attributed to the
problems with the *Mona's Isle* and passenger arrivals had dropped by
13.7%. Services on the Heysham route were reduced to two per day
until the end of May 1986, with no overnight Saturday sailings. At
the end of September the *Peveril* returned to resume an overnight
freight service, leaving daytime services with the *Tynwald* – a
combination which continued until February 1990. That basic
pattern of services was to continue until the introduction of the *Ben-
my-Chree* [6] in 1998. The integration of the two operations and cost

*Sealink's **Dalriada** in Douglas on 31st December 1979. (Stan Basnett)*

reduction requirements, needed to get the company back on an even
keel, did not go smoothly and there were four strikes during the
autumn of 1986.

As the Steam Packet struggled to return to profitability Industrial
action continued through to spring 1988. This led to Jim Sherwood,
the Sea Containers President, announcing that the Channel Islands
vessel *Earl Godwin* would sent to cover the 1988 TT race period –
but this never happened as the Isle of Man Government chartered
the *Bolette* from Fred Olsen. This was an unhappy period for all
concerned and the Isle of Man Government, who still held 8.15% of
the Steam Packet shares, had commissioned Wallems to advise them
on "Sea Transport to the Island". The report was published in May

*The **Manx Viking** arriving in Douglas on 28th July 1982. (John Hendy)*

*A rare photograph of the **Mona's Isle** [6] at sea. (Stan Basnett)*

*The **Mona's Queen**, **Stena Sailer** and **Manx Viking** in Heysham on 3rd April 1985. The **Stena Sailer** was on charter to Belfast Freight Ferries but was blocking the only linkspan in protest at being replaced by the **Peveril**. The Isle of Man service was therefore being maintained by the side-loading **Mona's Queen**. (M J Borrowdale)*

1988 but, despite being widely criticised, two of its recommendations were acted on – that the Manx Government dispose of its shareholding in the Steam Packet and take control of the linkspans in Douglas Harbour. At the time it was envisaged that the latter would, if necessary, be achieved by compulsory purchase - although that is not quite how things turned out.

During this period the *Tynwald* normally operated from the Victoria Pier and the *Peveril* from the Edward Pier, but on 14th July 1989 the *Peveril*'s starboard variable pitch propeller mechanism jammed, causing the ship to continue astern into the ramp, causing considerable damage. The linkspan had to be towed to the Mersey for repairs and until it returned on 30th November both ships had to use the Victoria Pier linkspan. By now there were severe congestion problems due to inadequate traffic marshalling areas and to provide

some relief the Circus Beach area, between Imperial Buildings (the Steam Packet Head Office) and the roadway between the two piers, was filled in to provide a weighbridge and hardstanding for trailers awaiting shipment.

**Resumption of rail services to Heysham**

In summer 1987 passenger rail services were restored to Heysham Harbour after a lapse of 12 years. The track had been retained for the movement of nuclear flasks for the Heysham Power Station and was still signalled to passenger standards, but signalling changes were

*The **Ben-my-Chree** (5) was sold and laid up at the end of the 1984 season, never having visited Heysham. Finding themselves short of capacity for the 1985 TT season, the Steam Packet chartered her back and put her briefly on the Heysham - Douglas service. Here the 'Ben' is seen berthing on 25th May at Heysham's North Quay. (John Hendy)*

planned which would have reduced it to freight only. There was therefore some reluctance on the part of the railway to re-open the link in case it was successful - and they then had to close it again because funds could not be found to re-signal it - or alternatively in case it failed and they then had to go through a statutory closure procedure. The first problem was overcome by the IOM Government, the Steam Packet and Lancashire County/Lancaster City Councils putting up funds to cover the extra costs of re-signalling to passenger standards.

Trains and crews had to be found to work the service. Regional Railways had just been established and had an imaginative train planner who identified diesel multiple units (DMUs) which were used only on rush hour services to the south of Manchester and which were therefore available to cover middle of the day arrivals and departures from Heysham. Thus when the service started one of the trains was a through working from Buxton to Heysham Harbour. The summer practice was to have two trains - one to connect with the arrival of the incoming ship, whilst a second brought passengers to the port for the afternoon sailing. The service was better supported than had been anticipated and although through workings from Manchester were discontinued the service became permanent.

## 1990 – 1999

In July 1994 a new link road from Heysham port to the western outskirts of Lancaster was opened so that at last it was possible for the port traffic to avoid running through built-up areas of

*The **Mona's Isle** turning in Heysham Harbour. (Dave Hocquard)*

Morecambe and Heysham for at least part of the journey to the M6. Unfortunately it was still necessary to go through the edge of the Lancaster City Centre. Although plans have been drawn up for a relief road direct to the M6 south of Lancaster – avoiding the conurbation completely, there seems no immediate prospect of this much-needed road being built

As the single linkspan in Heysham - dating from 1970 - was inadequate to handle the traffic which developed from the expanding services using the port, a second was built which opened in October 1995. This was a floating pontoon going out into the harbour from the east end, with vessels mooring on the south side of a new set dolphins built in the centre of the harbour.

In 1996 Fishers pulled their cargo handling out of Heysham but their local management took over providing services under the name North Lancashire Stevedores, but this operation only lasted a short time. A third linkspan was installed in 1997 to the north of No 2, with vessels mooring on the opposite side of the same dolphins. This was the ex IOM Steam Packet Navire linkspan which had been on the south side of the King Edward Pier in Douglas, so was already owned by Sea Containers. It had originally been designed to lie alongside a pier, so modifications were undertaken to enable traffic to run straight onto it. With the majority of the port's freight now going over the linkspans at the eastern end of the harbour, rather than via the traditional quays, it was necessary to open up that area for lorry and trailer parking.

The Fish Quay re-opened in the early 1990s, again handling sea dredged aggregate. The ships discharge using conveyors and the previously unused area immediately to the east of that is used as a bulk storage area.

The **Tynwald** at Heysham in 1986. The former **Antrim Princess** was on charter to the Steam Packet Company from Sea Containers between late 1985 and early 1990. (David Dixon)

## Growth in the Manx trade

With freight traffic increasing and trim problems with the *Tynwald*, the Steam Packet decided to replace her with the larger *Channel Entente* which undertook berthing trials early in January 1990 before being purchased the following month and taking up service on 19th February 1990. The new ship was better known as the cross-Channel ferry *Saint Eloi* and after a refit the following autumn was renamed *King Orry*. She was the first Steam Packet ship to be painted white since the 1930s. Her arrival necessitated further dredging to deepen Douglas Harbour to allow a minimum of 5 metres of water at all states of the tide. This work was undertaken in March 1990 by the PVW backhoe dredger *Skua* with spoil being

*In 1985 the Heysham booking hall was re-vamped in "Steam Packet Seaways" style.*

removed by the split hopper *Cork Sand*.

In June 1990 Sea Containers made a hostile bid to take complete control of the Steam Packet Company but the following month a bill was introduced in the House of Keys which would have prevented Sea Containers from increasing their holding in the company – or anyone else holding more than 15% unless approved by the Isle of Man Treasury. Despite the fact that the Bill was not passed into law, Sea Containers did not renew their bid.

## The IOM linkspan user agreement

Although the Douglas breakwater had been completed in 1983, the Steam Packet had not been required to move their linkspan to the north side of the Edward Pier but during the negotiations for its possible sale to the Government, formal notice was given that the agreement for siting the linkspan which was due to expire on 30th April 1991 would not be renewed. Subsequently a two and a half year extension was granted to allow negotiations to proceed and in December 1993 agreement was reached in principle for the sale of the Steam Packet's Douglas Navire linkspan on the Edward Pier to the Department of Highways, Ports and Properties, although the company would retain almost exclusive user rights. The Company would also contract to run specified minimum levels of service and hold fare increases to slightly below the rate of inflation. However by May 1994 the Manx Government had decided that, rather than proceed with the purchase of the Steam Packet's linkspan, they would build a new one of their own at a cost of £4 million. At the same time some serious efforts had been made to improve facilities for passengers in Douglas with the major refurbishment and upgrading of the barn-like public areas of the Sea Terminal and the covered walkways onto the Victoria Pier. Even a covered gangway for boarding the *King Orry* was provided.

The new Douglas harbour "government linkspan", on the north side of the Edward Pier came into operation on 1st October 1995 and with it the linkspan user agreement between the IOM Government and the Steam Packet. The main rights and obligations contained in the final, agreement were as follows:

1. The Government grants the Steam Packet Company sole user rights on the new Government owned linkspan subject to a restricted number of specialist, one-off and non-Company services. Government will extend the Company's licence to site the Victoria Pier linkspan for the initial term of the agreement.

2. In return for the security offered by Government undertakings, the Company will guarantee:

● Minimum levels of service based closely on existing schedules.

● Minimum levels of investment totalling £14 million over the first seven years of the agreement and £20 million over the first ten years, such figures to be adjusted for inflation, and spent on vessels employed on Isle of Man routes.

● Overall fare level increases above the Manx Retail Price Index less 0.5% may be subjected to independent binding arbitration at the Government's request. (Certain other issues relating to the agreement may, if appropriate, be subject to independent binding arbitration at the request of either party).

*The **Channel Entente** took over the Heysham – Isle of Man passenger service on 19th February 1990. After a major re-fit she was re-named **King Orry** the following December. She is seen here leaving Heysham in 1990. (John Hendy)*

The agreement was for an initial period of 10 years with the option for either party to extend the agreement for a further 5 years.

As part of the new linkspan project the outer harbour in Douglas between the two piers had been partially infilled to provide a proper marshalling area from which traffic could be directed to either linkspan, although normally the *King Orry* used the Victoria Pier linkspan as that berth had foot passenger access. Freight was handled by the *Peveril* on the new berth but at various times the *Belard,* which the company had bought for their ill-fated Mannin Line operation on the North Sea was substituted. Freight capacity to the Island was by now becoming a problem and as a matter of prudence it was decided that the new berth should be capable of handling the largest ships thought likely to use the harbour. As dredging alongside the pier could not be accomplished without jeopardising the foundations, mooring dolphins were provided parallel with the pier and braced back to it. This made gangway access to a vessel from the pier extremely difficult – but as only ro-ro freight was being handled this was not regarded as a problem.

## Sea Containers take over the Steam Packet

In Spring 1996, and with the User Agreement safely in place, Sea Containers launched another bid to take full control of the Steam Packet Company, and this time received the backing of the Directors and the company became a wholly owned subsidiary. Whilst the company name was retained, Imperial Buildings in Douglas became the HQ for Sea Containers Irish Sea Operations which, as well as the Steam Packet, comprised SeaCat Scotland, the Port of Heysham and for a short period the Argyll & Antrim Steam Packet Co. (which ran a service between Ballycastle and Campbeltown).

*The **Peveril** and **Channel Entente** at Douglas Harbour in 1990. (John Hendy)*

Summer 1998 saw major changes in the Isle of Man services with the introduction of the ro-pax *Ben-my-Chree* on 11th July 1998. She replaced both the *King Orry*, which made her last sailing on 28th September, on the passenger service and the *Peveril* on the freight run, thereby providing two sailings a day in each direction. Her passenger capacity at 350 was in practice only about a third of the *King Orry's*, although she was certificated for 500. The new Steam Packet management increased the frequency of services and introduced promotional fares to encourage travel by sea to and from the Island. After decades of decline, passenger growth was back on the agenda – aided by a booming Manx economy.

## Changes in Douglas

These changes provided new challenges for the port management in Douglas. The *Ben-my-Chree* at 125 metres long was 10 metres longer than the *King Orry* (and 19 metres more than the *Peveril*) and she was to carry both foot passengers as well as cars and freight. She was the first new ship built specifically for the Douglas – Heysham service since the *Manxman* of 1904 and she was probably built to the maximum size which could be accommodated on the new linkspan berth. Her gross tonnage at 12,504 dwarfed the *King Orry's* 7,555 and the 5,284 of the *Peveril*. Once it had been determined that she was to operate from the Government linkspan the immediate question was how foot passengers were to be moved between the ship and the passenger check-in facilities the opposite side of the harbour. The new ship loaded all her wheeled traffic over the stern but her passenger accommodation and access doors were all forward and it was necessary to keep foot passenger and vehicle movements separate.

This led to the erection of the overhead passenger walkway from the Sea Terminal to the base of the Edward Pier and a covered walkway along most of the length of the Edward Pier. The overhead section enabled passengers to cross above the traffic lanes to both linkspans and access was via steps in a tower at each end (with a lift being provided for the less fit). Fortunately the Steam Packet by now operated a check-in system for heavy baggage so passengers only had their hand luggage to carry, and the disabled were taken aboard by mini-bus. As built, the overhead section crosses the harbour with two support columns onto the harbour bed. The IOM Government insurers perceived a

*The **Ben-my-Chree** turning in Douglas Harbour in summer 1998. The **King Orry**, which she replaced, is unusually berthed on the outside of the Victoria Pier. (Miles Cowsill)*

risk that a manoeuvring vessel could collide with these columns, as a result of which no passengers are allowed to use the walkways while a vessel is entering the harbour and being made secure alongside.

*Seatruck Ferries started their Warrenpoint service with the chartered* **Bolero**, *here seen at Heysham in July 1996. (Ian Harmsworth)*

*The* **Saga Moon** *has served both the Belfast and Dublin routes from Heysham since her introduction by Belfast Freight Ferries in 1986. She is seen here carrying a short-lived paint scheme in June 1994.(Ian Harmsworth)*

The area opposite the *Ben-my-Chree*'s passenger shell doors has been decked to enable a gangway to be handled, near to the end of the covered walkway.

## Growth in Irish services

1991 saw the arrival in October of the *Schiaffino* as third ship for BFF, and Merchant Ferries added a second ship to their Warrenpoint service. In 1993 BFF's *Schiaffino* was replaced by the *River Lune* and the Merchant Ferries' Warrenpoint service went up to a three ship operation with the purchase of the *Merchant Brilliant* and *Merchant Bravery*, to run alongside the *Merchant Venture*. In 1995 Merchant Ferries switched their Warrenpoint service to Dublin and in October 1996 the *Merle* came in on charter to BFF.

In 1998 Cenargo started expanding rapidly. They first took over Scruttons, the parent company of BFF and in 1999 BFF was absorbed into Merchant Ferries. They also opened a ro-pax service from Liverpool to Dublin which had some detrimental effect on their loadings out of Heysham and acquired the Belfast – Liverpool operator Norse Irish Ferries the same year, adding further tonnage to that route.

Merchant Ferries' move to Dublin proved the catalyst for some of their disaffected staff, backed by Crescent Shipping Plc, to set up Seatruck Ferries in 1996 to re-open the Warrenpoint service. Starting with the chartered Romanian vessel *Bolero, they* then took on the *Eurobridge* from Sally Ferries (which had been the *Schiaffino* used by BFF five years earlier) and renamed her as the *Riverdance*, purchasing the ship in 1997. They also chartered sister ship the *Merchant Victor* from Cenargo in 1997, renaming her the *Moondance,* and purchased her the following year.

69

*The **Ben-my-Chree** arriving in Heysham after her morning sailing from Douglas. (Miles Cowsill)*

*The **Hoverspeed Great Britain** which operated the Belfast-Heysham service in 2001. (Author's photo)*

## The Belfast – Heysham passenger service returns

In March 1999 Sea Containers decided to re-open the Heysham – Belfast passenger service using the fast craft *SeaCat Danmark* which could carry both cars and passengers and provided a four-hour transit. Two sailings a day were offered in the peak season. At the Belfast end the vessel ran from the SeaCat terminal at Donegall Quay which was already used by SeaCat Scotland for the service to Stranraer (later Troon), as well as for Belfast – Isle of Man sailings. This terminal was on the site of the historic railway steamer berth, but had been built in 1970 for the Heysham car ferry service.

## THE 21ST CENTURY

Duringthe first three years of the 21st Century, the ownership of Heysham Port and all of its main shipping customers changed. In each case there were only minimal changes in the management of the operations concerned and vessels deployed. The outcome appears to be very much "business as usual".

### Mersey Docks buy Heysham Port

In May 2001 Sea Containers sold Heysham Port to the Mersey Docks Group. The great advantage of this move was that the port was now owned by a professional and expansion-minded port management company, whilst still benefiting from a continuity in

*The **Saga Moon** leaving Heysham in NMF colours. (Author's photo)*

*The **Merchant Brilliant** of NorseMerchant Ferries at Heysham No 2 linkspan in February 2004. (Author's photo)*

metre *Seacat Danmark* (1999) and the *Hoverspeed Great Britain* were probably too small for comfort on a four hour voyage. The larger and very different *SuperSeaCat Two* and the *Rapide* both suffered major technical problems which necessitated early closure of the service. One of the major problems with operating this as a fast craft route was the lack of any nearby conventional service to which passengers could be transferred in the event of cancellations for technical or weather reasons. It is uncertain whether the route will re-open for passengers.

In 2001 all the Irish Sea operations which Cenargo had acquired were brought together under the NorseMerchant Ferries brand but by early 2003 the group were in major financial difficulties which resulted in a reduction of services on most of their routes and a restructuring in which the Cenargo name disappeared and the

*The **River Lune** in Belfast Freight Ferries colours at Heysham in May 1995. (Author's photo)*

local management. One of the first visible benefits of new ownership was a programme of investment involving the pouring of large quantities of concrete and the purchase of a new fleet of Tugmasters. The other major change arose from the fact that the new owners of the port had their own dredgers which took over the work of harbour and channel dredging, with the *Mersey Venture* often being deployed to Heysham.

## Irish Services from Heysham

The Belfast seasonal car and passenger service was operated by the *SuperSeaCat Two* in 2000, but she was replaced by the smaller *Hoverspeed Great Britain* in 2001. In 2002 yet another fast craft was used, the *Rapide* but no service was provided in 2003. Both the 74

holding company became Norse Merchant Group. What had earlier been a six ship fleet based at Heysham was reduced to four vessels although March 2004 saw the resumption of a three ship service to Belfast.

Most of the Heysham vessels operated by NorseMerchant are approaching 25 years old. They have not previously invested in new tonnage for freight only operations and the length limitations on turning in Heysham Harbour (about 140 metres) would seriously limit their choice of second hand replacement tonnage. NorseMerchant, before their parent company Cenargo got into financial difficulties, had been talking of new builds for the Heysham route, but it is now almost certain that the new management will revive this plan.

The **Ben-my-Chree** at No2 linkspan and the **Rapide** at No1 on 19th March 2002. The **Rapide** was undertaking ramp trials before taking up the Belfast – Heysham service. (Ian Harmsworth)

The **Lady of Mann** lying at Heysham's North Quay during her TT service in May 2003. (Author's photo)

The Seatruck Ferries twice daily freight service to Warrenpoint continues using the *Moondance* and the *Riverdance*. The service had to be diverted to Larne between 5th January and 5th February 2002, following the failure of the hydraulics on the only linkspan at Warrenpoint on 4th January. In May the same year the *European Mariner*, sister to the *Moondance* and *Riverdance*, was chartered from P&O to cover a two week refit on the *Riverdance*. Their parent company Crescent Shipping was taken over in 2002 by the Bahamas based Clipper Group but this made no apparent difference to their day to day operation. Their vessels are now over 25 years old and whilst their modest length (116.3 metres) makes them ideal for Warrenpoint there would be no difficulty in replacing them with slightly longer ships at some future time.

In Spring 2004 the P&O service to Larne from nearby Fleetwood was taken over by Stena. The Irish Sea freight market had

*The **SuperSeaCat Two** speeds out of Morecambe Bay en route for Belfast on 21st June 2000. (Author's photo)*

stabilised following a period of over expansion followed by retrenchment and there were some cautious signs of improving volumes and returns. Fleetwood services will require further investment within a short number of years if they are to survive and remain a challenge to those from Heysham.

## Heysham – Isle of Man

At peak times from 2000 onwards the *Ben-my-Chree* was backed up by a limited number of sailings by the *Seacat Isle of Man*. During her refits in 2000, 2002 and 2004 her passenger sailings were covered by the car ferry *Lady of Mann* and the freight carried on chartered freight ro-ro vessels – *Dart 1* (2000) *Belard* and *European Mariner* (2002) and *Hoburgen* (2004). As part of her spring 2004 refit the *Ben-*

*my-Chree* was fitted with additional passenger accommodation which increased her effective capacity from 350 to 500. The company has a commitment to the Isle of Man Government to progressively increase its freight capacity up to the year 2010. It is unclear whether this might be achieved by new tonnage to either supplement or replace the 'Ben' or whether passenger/car traffic would be encouraged to use the Liverpool services, thus freeing up more space for freight.

The *Lady of Mann's* other role on the Heysham service has been in the early summer to carry large numbers of motor cycles and their riders to the Isle of Man for the TT races. As a side-loader she operates independently of link spans and can use most of the berths in the harbour to which vehicular access is available. Initially she

*The **Belard** was chartered by the Steam Packet in January 2002 whilst the **Ben-my-Chree** was under refit. She later served on the Caledonian MacBrayne Stornaway-Ullapool service as the **Muirneag**. (Author's photo)*

*The stern view shows clearly the extension work to the passenger accommodation which was undertaken to **Ben-my-Chree** in January 2004. (Miles Cowsill)*

used the North Quay – with passengers being 'bussed' round, but later she was accommodated adjacent to the passenger terminal on the South Quay. With modifications to the No 1 linkspan and, subsequently, new access gangways for the *Ben-my-Chree*, vehicle access was impeded and the 'Lady's' usual berth is now in the middle of the South Quay – with foot passengers again being transferred to and from the terminal by bus.

## The Steam Packet is sold

In March 2002 the Douglas Harbour Linkspan User Agreement was extended to 2010 with some modification to the terms to increase the guaranteed levels of service and freight capacity as well as to secure "special offer fares" on a permanent basis. By then Sea Containers were suffering cash flow problems which were preventing further investment in the Isle of Man operation and they used the extension of the agreement as security for a substantial cash raising exercise, of which about half was to have been for the benefit of the Steam Packet Company. On 30th June 2003 Sea Containers sold

*The Travel Shop in the Sea Terminal at Douglas handles Steam Packet bookings and enquiries. (Author's photo)*

*The Seacat terminal at Donegall Quay, Belfast uses the facilities built in 1970 for the Sealink Heysham Car Ferry. It is used by services to Troon and the Isle of Man as well as the service to Heysham which ran between 1999 and 2002. (Author's photo)*

their entire shareholding in the Steam Packet to Montagu Private Equity who retained the existing management team

## Douglas Harbour

Future developments in Douglas are likely to depend on the need to handle bigger ships. The current Edward Pier berth used by the *Ben-my-Chree* (125 metres long) would not be able to handle a significantly longer vessel. Allowing for the ship to swing inside the harbour the maximum turning circle that could be provided would probably be 160 metres —enough for a 140 metre long ship. A ship of this length could only be accommodated at the Victoria Pier, but if double deck loading were required the linkspan would need to be

moved further down the pier to enable top deck traffic to pass under the existing pedestrian walkway. Thus if the Victoria Pier linkspan — originally provided by Manx Line and now much modified — is to be replaced, it could not sensibly be in the existing position. Such a move would allow more infill between the Victoria and Edward Piers, thus increasing the amount of hardstanding available, but would have the disadvantage of loosing a berth on the inside of the Victoria Pier.

The tanker traffic in Douglas is now in decline. In the later part of the 20th century the Isle of Man imported all its gas and generated all its electricity from imported oil, most of which came in through the tanker terminal at the Battery Pier. By 2002 a power

Heysham run would dictate any change in these ports. In both ports substantial expansion and modernisation programmes are in progress which will mean the ports continuing to be developed seaward and the re-development of the older port areas for non shipping business.

Warrenpoint has regularly handled ro-ro ships up to 140 metres in the past – the main problem being turning space should larger vessels than the current 116 metre long pair be put on the service. This would require ships turning at the head of the lough rather than in the river as at present but there would be no major development needed to handle bigger ships.

*Most ships are usually in Heysham Harbour on Sundays as many freight services only run overnight at weekends. Here the **Saga Moon** and Seatruck Ferries' **Riverdance** - with her short lived pale blue hull – take a Sunday off in July 2001. (Author's photo)*

cable had been commissioned from the Fylde coast to connect into the UK National Grid and the Island's main power station. Subsequently the Manx Electricity Authority completed a new power station powered by natural gas which was imported by pipeline. Gas from this pipeline is also used to supply the domestic market in the Douglas area.

## Irish ports

In Belfast, Victoria Terminal 1, from which the NorseMerchant Heysham service runs can accommodate ships of up to 155 metres and their Dublin berth is of similar length. It would therefore appear unlikely that any different ships they might introduce on the

*The 1970 passenger terminal at Heysham is situated on the South Quay immediately alongside the No 1 linkspan berth used by Isle of Man and Warrenpoint sailings. (Author's photo)*

# Sailing the Douglas – Heysham Route – by Captain Ken Crellin

*Captain Ken Crellin*

Captain Ken Crellin, who has written this chapter, retired as co-ordinating master of the Steam Packet Company flagship Ben-my-Chree in 2002, after 40 years at sea. Manx-born and educated he served an apprenticeship with Elder Dempster Lines in the West African trade. On completion of his training he obtained his Second Mates' certificate and joined the Steam Packet Company in February 1966. For his first six weeks with the company he served as an Able Seaman on the *Mona's Isle* but within two years had passed his Master's examination and then went on to take his Liverpool Pilotage examination.

In 1978 he was invited to join the new Manx Line operation as captain of the *Manx Viking*. Having seen that ro-ro was the way forward and established that the Steam Packet had no plans to move in this direction Ken accepted the offer and stayed with the *Manx Viking* from her delivery voyage from Leith until she was withdrawn from service after the merger between Sealink-Manx Line and the Steam Packet in 1984. Once the *Manx Viking* had been withdrawn,

Captains Ray Dickinson and Ken Crellin on the bridge of the **Manx Viking** on the completion of her delivery voyage from Leith in August 1978.

Ken served as master on the *Tynwald* and then the *Channel Entente*, which replaced her and was re-commissioned after a major re-fit as the *King Orry* and later Ken became her senior captain. He has unrivalled experience as master of sailing in and out of Heysham over nearly quarter of a century.

In 1994 he took a short break from the Heysham route when the Steam Packet chartered the *Seacat Isle of Man* for an initial two year trial period. Before taking command he undertook three months of training in high-speed navigation and ship systems and was in command on her maiden voyage from Douglas to Fleetwood.

Masters and officers during the final week of the **Manx Viking's** Isle of Man service in September 1986. (back row) Roger Jackson, Capt Mike Leadley, Chris Kneale, Geoff Quine (purser) and Roger Moore. (front) Captain Jack Woods, Dermot O'Toole, Captain Ken Crellin. All were to go on to serve in the Steam Packet Company, and Roger Moore and Dermot O'Toole both became captains.

Since the delivery of the *Ben-my-Chree* in 1988 Ken has been one of the four captains regularly in command of the vessel and even came out of retirement in 2003 and 2004 to help during the peak season.

## GEOGRAPHY

The ferry route between Douglas and Heysham consists essentially of a 49 mile open sea passage, and a more enclosed but navigationally demanding 10 mile leg into Morecambe Bay and Heysham port. The sea passage is straightforward from the navigator's point of view with few hazards except the rigs of Morecambe Bay Gas Field, which lies about five miles south of the main route. Depths are fairly shallow, averaging about 30 to 40 metres – less, indeed, than the distance from keel to masthead of a large ferry – but this depth is ample for normal navigation.

The sea bottom is fairly flat, consisting mostly of sand and fragmented shells with very few rocky outcrops. Approaching the Lune Buoy, the character of the area changes, the first evidence of this being visible on the ship's echo sounder (best seen when north of the buoy) as a precipitous drop from the 10 metre flats into an enormous 80 metre hole, scoured by the tide as it sweeps in and out of Morecambe Bay twice a day. From there, however, as the ship heads north eastwards into the bay, the channel begins to narrow (from a mile at the bay entrance to only a few hundred feet in the approaches to Heysham) and depths steadily decrease to less than five metres in the port approaches with the bottom becoming progressively more muddy. As a large ferry like the *Ben-my-Chree* draws over five and a half metres, it can be seen that the extra depth provided by the rise and fall of the

tide is an extremely important factor.

On the return journey, as the ship approaches the Isle of Man, the area takes on a markedly different character. The rocky coastline rises steeply out of the sea surrounding Douglas Harbour entrance. Depth of water is not a great problem here, although any serious misjudgement in the line of approach, of course, would have more damaging consequences.

### Tides

Tides in the Morecambe Bay area rise and fall up to ten metres in height and often flow at rates of five knots or more into the bay and across the entrance to Heysham Harbour – a crucial feature of the approach to the port. Entering Heysham with a strong flood tide running is not for the faint-hearted and is a skill only acquired after months of training. The vessel cannot 'stem the tide' in the traditional way but must approach with the tide behind her, turning at right angles to it at the last moment to enter the harbour. This manoeuvre requires precise judgement and is never taken lightly, even on a fine day, but it soon becomes second nature to the experienced Master.

Douglas is affected to a lesser degree but here too, the tidal flow runs across the harbour entrance and must be taken into account – particularly in fog, which we will consider later. The time of high (and low) water advances about one hour later each day and is one of the few precisely predictable events in the marine world. Tidal movement is a consequence of the gravitational effects of sun and moon, and times of high water calculated years in advance will vary by only a few minutes on the day. Heights are also calculated, but can sometimes vary by a metre or more, due to atmospheric pressure and storm surges.

The scheduled arrival times of the *Ben-my-Chree* are around midday

*The **Manx Viking** with Heysham Nuclear Power Station behind. (John Hendy)*

*The **Ailsa Princess** at the Victoria Pier in Douglas – winter 1981/2. (Ken Crellin collection)*

and midnight. If high water occurs at about that time, the inward voyage will have the benefit of the fast-running flood tide and the return passage, two hours later, will benefit from the ebb tide, which will by then be running in the opposite direction. Thus, fast passages in both directions will be observed several days in succession, until the high water time advances to late afternoon, and creating the opposite effect and slowing the vessel.

Incidentally, contrary to belief in some quarters, the ship is never run slowly to save fuel – the engines are designed and built to run at full speed and always do so. Reductions are only made for navigational safety (fog, for example) or port traffic control.

## WEATHER

### Gales

The Irish Sea has acquired something of a reputation for unpleasant sea conditions, due to its southern approaches being open to the prevailing winds. Whilst this is quite true and heavy seas can sometimes be encountered, gales are surprisingly rare and (sometimes to our own surprise) entire winters have been known to pass without a single day of gale force conditions being recorded by the Met.Office. Normally, however, we get our share, and wind strength is a major factor when manoeuvring the vessel in and out of port. At each end of the voyage, the ship must be turned completely round to enable berthing stern-

*The **Manx Viking** turning in Heysham Harbour in December 1981. The rig **Western Apollo** is in harbour for repair. (Photo by Peter Joslin. Courtesy of Lancaster City Museums)*

*SNCF's **Villandry** arrives at Heysham on charter to Sealink Manx Line in 1983. (Courtesy of Lancaster City Museums)*

but there are common sense limits which the Master must consider. Passenger comfort is foremost among these – in extreme weather, injuries could occur to those unused to vessel movement and valuable cargo could be damaged – freight vehicles are always well chained to the vessel, but the possibility of items moving *inside* their sealed containers must also be considered. There is also little point in making a difficult and uncomfortable passage if conditions are likely to preclude safe berthing at the other end. Also, however unlikely it may be, the Master must weigh the possibility of an emergency developing at sea, and the ability of his safety teams to cope in heavy weather.

first, and must be brought beam-on to the wind for a crucial few minutes. At this stage, the bow thrusters (a sideways mounted propeller in the bow) must be powerful enough to hold the vessel safely in position until she is berthed. If the wind is too strong (westerly in Heysham or easterly in Douglas), this cannot be safely achieved and the Master must wait until conditions improve. Fortunately, this circumstance is also infrequent – although all Masters will testify to the high stress level when it does occur!

On the open sea passage, the heavy sea and swell produced by a (usually South Westerly) gale is the factor which must be considered. The ship herself is designed to cope safely with virtually any sea conditions and the cargo is always properly secured for every voyage,

*Townsend-Thoresen's **Viking III** was on charter to Sealink - Manx Line in 1980. She is seen here arriving at Heysham on 29th February 1980. (Ian Harmsworth)*

## Fog

At the other end of the weather scale, fog can affect the route at any time of year. A modern ferry is usually fitted with at least two gyro-stabilised radars, a satellite positioning system and good VHF radio communications with ports and other vessels. Normally, the Master and Duty Navigating Officer will man one radar each, one concentrating on collision avoidance and the other on general navigation. Speed will be adjusted according to the conditions. Movements of all radar targets are carefully plotted by the radar operator and the vessel manoeuvred to maintain safe passing distances, following the strict requirements of the 'Collision Regulations' – a set of international rules which every Navigating Officer must know by heart.

Entry into the ports of Heysham and Douglas in fog requires special skill. Wind and tidal effects on the vessel are uncertain factors which cannot (yet) be accurately enough measured by instrumentation, and the ship's line of approach must be carefully monitored by the experienced eye of the Master. Douglas can usually be entered at any time, as the tidal flow is not unduly strong, but Heysham must be treated with great care, as tidal rates of five knots or more run directly across the entrance. In fog, a cautious approach can sometimes be made with the vessel proceeding slowly against the ebb tide (never flood) until a visual sighting of the entrance is made, but if the visibility is very poor, all cautious Masters will await high or low water, when the tide slackens. Even so, there are occasions when fog is so dense that no safe entry can be made, but fortunately such conditions are usually encountered only once every few years.

All of these weather considerations must be judged by the Master as he examines the latest forecast before every voyage. If a delay or cancellation is necessary, every Captain is painfully aware of the inconvenience to passengers and freight customers, but will never allow commercial considerations to influence safety decisions.

## THE HUMAN ELEMENT

### Crew

A modern passenger/freight ferry costs several tens of millions of pounds to build, but without a competent and efficient crew, of course, she will not earn a penny in return. For each voyage, the *Ben-my-Chree* has a crew of at least twenty-eight seafarers. This is the minimum

*On 23rd October 1998, soon after being withdrawn from Steam Packet service, the* **King Orry** *left Birkenhead under the Italian flag bearing the name* **Moby Love**. *(John Shepherd)*

*Harbour Control monitors vessel movements at Douglas. (Author's photo)*

*The **Peveril** leaving Douglas on her final service sailing to Heysham on 10th July 1998. (Jenny Williamson)*

number required to cope with any reasonably foreseeable emergency and is determined by the Marine Administration of the 'Flag State' (The Isle of Man in our case). For good passenger service, more than this number is usually carried.

The Master, as always, remains in overall charge of the three traditional departments – deck, engine and catering. The deck department is responsible for navigation and cargo operations, and consists of two officers and ten seamen. Machinery and technical matters are the responsibility of the Chief Engineer, assisted by three engineer officers, an electrician and two motormen. Passengers are looked after by the Customer Services Officer and ten (sometimes more) ratings.

The ship operates for twenty-four hours a day, every day, so four crews are required, each working a seven-day week of twelve-hour shifts, changing at 07.00 and 19.00, followed by a week off. Extras are needed to cover leave and sickness, although the latter is surprisingly uncommon on board ship – annual fitness examinations are required for all crew and the culture of seafaring has always frowned on absence for minor snuffles and melancholy!

## Training

Every crew member requires a strictly determined level of training, set by the marine authorities and all ships are frequently inspected to ensure compliance. All deck and engineer officers must be examined and certificated, usually by the Maritime and Coastguard Agency (MCA) – a multi-stage process which takes an average of ten years or more before an officer is permitted to take sole charge of the deck or engine department on board.

In addition, the Master must be examined and licensed by the various Port Authorities to pilot his vessel in their areas - Heysham, Liverpool, Belfast and Dublin are all examples. Unlike aviation, ship movements are not directed to any great degree by shore controllers, and the responsibility for safe pilotage and collision avoidance in these complex areas falls mainly on the Master. (In some of the larger ports a greater degree of shore control is now becoming more common).

Ratings too, must be trained and examined to ensure their competence (also by the Maritime & Coastguard Agency in the case of safety duties). This involves a wide range of skills, from launching and

*The **Ben-my-Chree** making her final turn through the roundheads at the end of another voyage from Douglas in April 2000. (Author's photo)*

recovery of the ship's lifeboats to refuelling operations and galley hygiene. Every detail of this training is recorded and checked by the marine authorities – and there are unannounced, on-board inspections.

**The Working Day (or Night)**

To a casual observer, a ferry service may seem repetitive, but in reality, no two trips are the same. The night crew of the *Ben-my-Chree* will board about fifteen minutes before the official time of 19.00, in order to meet their opposite number in the day crew, and acquaint themselves with any ongoing business. A passage plan is prepared by the bridge officer for the Master's approval before every departure. The ever changing times and heights of tide must be considered, along with an up to the minute weather forecast (usually very accurate), provided by our great friends at Ronaldsway Met. Office. Passengers will be boarding at that time, and the Customer Services staff are all busy allocating cabins, manning service points and preparing meals.

In the Engine Room, essential systems will be checked and tested, fuel levels verified and auxiliary machinery run up ready for departure. Meanwhile, on the vehicle deck, the Loading Officer (one of the two deck officers), assisted by the duty seamen will be wrestling with a complex loading list, consisting of many different types of vehicles. Although the 'Ben' is a large vessel, special stowage areas must be set aside for hazardous goods, high vehicles, wide or heavy loads, refrigerated vehicles, motorcycles, late arrivals, passengers with special needs, and many others.

Juggling all these requirements is no easy matter but eventually, it all comes together and about ten minutes before sailing time the Loading Officer will inform the bridge that the stern door is closed and vehicle decks secure in all respects. This is a high-pressure period for the

*The **Ben-my-Chree** prior to her launch in Holland. (Ferry Publications Library)*

Bridge (Master, Bridge Officer and Helmsman) and Engine Control Room (Chief, Second and Third Engineer and Motorman) who must carry out a comprehensive checklist of all manoeuvring and safety systems, start and run up the main engines, steering and bow thrust units and verify that all working temperatures and pressures are correct. Finally, on the Bridge, the vessel's stability will be calculated, watertight doors checked and sailing clearance obtained from port control.

When the vessel has cleared Douglas and is settled on course for the Lune Buoy, provided the weather is satisfactory and there are no unusual dangers, both the Master and Chief Engineer will hand over the watch to one of their senior officers to enable them to catch up with the inevitable paperwork or other duties. Typically, this may include a safety meeting with other crew members, or perhaps a

formal vessel inspection, which must take place every week.

As the licensed pilot, the Master must take over the bridge again at the Lune Buoy, to navigate the complex channel into Heysham and the Chief Engineer will also return to his Control Room. Entering Heysham Harbour requires considerable concentration, particularly with a strong flood tide running. As the vessel turns across the tide, she will be 'slipping' some twenty or thirty degrees to the side of her line of approach, and very precise judgement is needed to place the vessel in the centre of the narrow entrance.

Vessel 'turnround' in Heysham will take around two hours, all outward passengers and cargo disembarking and the inward traffic being brought aboard. A feature of the night passage from Heysham is the freight load, which is always heavy – around a thousand tonnes, on average.

It is always interesting for a veteran like myself to recall the days of the nineteen sixties, when the combined load of *three* freight vessels in an entire week was little more than that figure! Although costs may have increased in real terms, there must be few industries which can show such an increase in productivity in thirty years.

## CHANGES

My own career on Irish Sea routes spans some thirty-five years and enormous changes have taken place in that time.

### Ships

Most passenger ships trading into the Port of Heysham in the nineteen sixties were still propelled by steam, although the diesel engine was making rapid inroads. Steam turbines were a powerful and reliable method of propulsion, but used large amounts of fuel and were slow to respond when manoeuvring – few ships had bow thrusts and handling required great skill.

Virtually all ferries are now diesel powered and have variable pitch propellers, twin rudders and bow thrust units. This extra manoeuvrability has its commercial collateral, of course – the ability to operate much larger ships, which are now around twice the tonnage of their equivalents thirty years ago.

## Administration

The paperwork which now lands on the desk of a modern shipmaster would surprise those of a generation ago. Every detail of crew training, drills, inspections, maintenance, incidents, checklists, stability calculations, meetings and much else besides, is now carefully recorded, signed and sent ashore for approval. The concept of 'Master Under God' (which never was quite true, of course, even in days of sail) is now a distant memory.

## Ports

The ports of Heysham and Douglas have both undergone great changes, many of which directly affect the handling and berthing of vessels. Heysham has been provided with two extra ro-ro berths in the centre of the harbour, greatly increasing the traffic potential, but reducing the manoeuvring area for vessels when turning to berth. This often precludes the traditional 'anchor swing' in high winds and makes the provision of powerful bow thrust units even more essential for regular traders. Douglas has been transformed by the addition of a new breakwater, protecting it from the easterly gales, which, in previous times would close the port for days on end.

## The Sea

For all this, the elements have not changed in the slightest. The journey may be short, but when the ship leaves Douglas and clears the breakwater, she is at sea and the approaching wave is made of exactly the same stuff as it's equivalent in mid-Atlantic. Preparations for a voyage to Heysham are, in fact, little different to those for New York or Valparaiso and great care is taken to ensure that safety is never compromised. The Steam Packet Company has an enviable record in this respect – perhaps due in some measure to its traditional Island base, which tends to encourage a steady, long-term workforce, familiar with every detail of their ships.

*The **Ben-my-Chree** approaches DouglasHarbour in June 2004. (Miles Cowsill)*

# Morecambe Bay Gasfield and Support Base

Gas had been discovered under the Irish Sea in 1974 and following this two developments took place which led to a change in the fortunes of the port of Heysham. On 1st December 1981 the exploration drilling rig Western Apollo II was towed into Heysham Harbour for repairs to damage sustained on passage from Singapore. Although the repairs only took a matter of weeks its presence in the harbour was a very visible symbol of renewed activity in the port. Of enormous significance for the future of Heysham port was the decision in 1982 by British Gas to establish their Morecambe Bay supply base at the harbour. Within 20 years the Morecambe Bay gas fields were capable of producing 15% of UK peak gas demand

The Morecambe Bay Gasfields are today operated by Hydrocarbon Resources Limited (HRL), a wholly owned subsidiary of Centrica plc – the parent company of British Gas. Over 400 staff and contractors work on the platforms, supply base and processing terminals, of whom about 143 are offshore at any time – although that number can increase if workload demands it, usually when summer maintenance is being carried out. There are beds for 170 in two-man cabins on the accommodation platform and a dining area

*Gulf Offshore's production support supply vessel* **Highland Pioneer** *at Heysham Harbour. (Author's picture)*

in which 100 can eat at any one time. Personnel going offshore are normally transported by helicopter from a dedicated terminal at Blackpool Airport although there is a helipad at the Heysham supply base.

The South Morecambe field was discovered in 1974 and covers an area of 32 square miles. Development started in 1979 but it was not until 8th January 1985 that the first gas came ashore. The opposite side of a deep geological fault, the smaller North Morecambe field (11 square miles) was found in 1976 but was only completed in October 1994. The top of the undersea gas reservoir is 900 metres below sea level gas – the sea itself being around 30 metres deep. The South Morecambe field consists of a central production complex with three bridge linked platforms for drilling, production and accommodation and a further four remote drilling platforms, which are not normally manned. Electrical power for the field is generated by four 3.2 megawatt Ruston (gas/diesel) turbines. The gas is piped from the remote platforms to the production complex for processing (gas/liquid separation and dehydration) and then, after compression, on to a terminal at Barrow in Furness through a 36 inch diameter pipeline. The compressors are driven by Rolls Royce RB211 gas turbines.

The North Morecambe gas is all processed ashore which means that the offshore drilling and production platform is normally unmanned, all operations being controlled from ashore. This is highly cost efficient as it means that complex machinery does not have to be installed and maintained offshore. As the gas from this field has a higher carbon dioxide and nitrogen content than that from the South Morecambe field it has to be piped and processed separately.

The Bains field is about eight miles NE of the South Morecambe field and produced its first gas in November 2002. It is operated from a subsea well head from which gas is piped undersea into the South Morecambe system. The only visible indication of the field at sea level is a marker buoy over the well.

## Millom, Dalton and Rivers fields

Although owned by Burlington Resources (Irish Sea) Limited, these fields are also operated by HRL, with the gas from the first two being fed to the North Morecambe platform and then to the North Morecambe terminal at Barrow in Furness. The Millom field uses the Millom West platform which is normally unattended,

*HRL operate the Calder Platform, south of the Morecambe Gasfields, on behalf of Burlington Resources.(picture courtesy British Gas Hydrocarbon Resources)*

whereas the Dalton field uses a subsea well linked to the same platform. The Rivers field was due to land its first gas early in 2004.

## The Heysham Gas Field support base

Hydrocarbons Great Britain, the company which was later to become British Gas Hydrocarbon Resources Limited (HRL) moved into temporary accommodation on site in July 1983. The first supply ship had already berthed on 29th May 1983. Work began to build the 22-acre supply base at the western end of the North Quay and this was fully operational two years later. The supply base consists of a 4,600 square metre mainly racked warehouse where engineering supplies of every type are stored – from turbines and pipework right through to electric light bulbs. It is also responsible for the supply of fuel for use on the platforms and the reception of all types of waste which is sent ashore for disposal. Fuel is normally brought in by coastal tanker and held in shore tanks until piped into the deep tanks on the supply vessels, although on occasion road tankers are used. All materials are picked from the warehouse and packed into a variety of containers which are carried out to the platform on the afterdeck of the supply boats. These containers are then craned off when the supply boat reaches the appropriate platform.

Although the supply boats carry out all the food and domestic supplies, most of these consumables arrive at the support base ready packed into the appropriate containers. The major supplier for these items is J C Altham who operate from a new warehouse adjacent to the port. Their business was established in 1856 to provide ships stores and as well as servicing the offshore industry they are active throughout the North West supplying the ferry industry.

By 1992 there were over 600 supply ship movements each year.

In 1999 BHP Petroleum (now BHP Billiton), operator of the Liverpool Bay oil and gas fields, combined their operational support with that of HRL, thereby providing a single supply structure for the Liverpool Bay and Morecambe Bay fields. With the base now carrying supplies for three different companies (the third being Burlington) the running of the base was put in the hands of Seaforth Maritime Ltd who are responsible for the marine scheduling and

*Seacore's jack-up rig **Excalibur**, seen here arriving in Heysham Harbour early in 2004, prior to starting construction work on the Barrow off-shore wind farm (David Fairclough)*

## RIGS SERVICED: (JAN 2004)

| | |
|---|---|
| HRL | CPC1,DP3, DP4, DP6, DP8, DPPA, Millom West and Calder Platform |
| BHP | Douglas, OS1, Hamilton, Hamilton North, Lennox platforms and Irish Sea Pioneer (Jack-up support rig) |
| BHP Drilling | Ensco85 (Drilling Rig) |
| Windfarm project | Seacore Excalibur (working from Heysham from end Feb 2004) |

**Production Support Supply Vessel**

| | |
|---|---|
| *Highland Pioneer* | (Gulf Offshore) |

**Emergency Response & Recovery Vessels, (ERRV).**

| | |
|---|---|
| BHP Billiton Liverpool Bay | *Grampian Supporter* (Boston Putford) |
| | *Clwyd Supporter* (Boston Putford) |
| HRL Morecambe Bay | *Highland Sprite* (Gulf Offshore) |

**Drilling Support**

| | |
|---|---|
| BHP Billiton | *Olympic Supplier* (Olympic Shipping) |

quayside activities of the dedicated supply vessel *Highland Pioneer* and for quayside activities for the drilling support vessel *Olympic Supplier*. Two such vessels (up to 80 metres long) can be handled at the North Quay berths. Henty Oil has the contract to provide bunkers for the supply boats. These are delivered by coastal tanker to the tank farm at the supply base about every six weeks – from whence they are pumped directly onto the vessel.

### Looking Forward

The Irish Sea gasfields are now past their peak production capacity and it is unlikely that further substantial development will prove possible or economic. Whether other forms of off-shore activity can replace this is doubtful but one pending development is the building of a windfarm 8 kilometres off-shore from Walney Island near Barrow, in which Centrica/British Gas will have a 25% stake. This will consist of 30 wind turbines and will be one of the largest offshore projects in the UK. Construction is likely to begin in 2004/5 but remains to be seen whether the Heysham offshore support base will be used to support the construction or maintenance of this facility. The UK Government has designated the Eastern Irish Sea as a major area for offshore windfarm development so there are real prospects for developing the port's role in this area.

*The assistance of Chris Nolan (Seaforth Maritime) Andrew Hanson (Centrica plc) and Tom Dodd (British Gas Hydrocarbon Resources) in compiling this section is gratefully acknowledged.*

# Appendix One

## BIBLIOGRAPHY

**Anon**: HEYSHAM HARBOUR ("Transport" Nov 1902)

**G N Abernethy**: MIDLAND RAILWAY's HARBOUR AT HEYSHAM (1903)

**W H Best**: HEYSHAM HARBOUR

**C Brown**: DOUGLAS HARBOUR WORKS - (1936)

**W P Clegg & J S Styring**: BRITISH NATIONALISED SHIPPING 1947-1968

**Miles Cowsill & John Hendy**: THE SEALINK YEARS 1970 - 1995

**(Sea Breezes** June 1955): FIFTY YEARS at HEYSHAM

**Duckworth & Langmuir**: RAILWAY & OTHER STEAMERS (1968)

**A M Goodwyn**: EIGHT DECADES of HEYSHAM DOUGLAS IS THIS ANY WAY TO RUN A SHIPPING LINE?

**John Hendy**: A MANX ENTERPRISE

**W B Kinley**: THE DEVELOPMENT OF DOUGLAS HARBOUR - (1992/3)

**R Lendrum-Aynsley**: THE METAMORPHOSIS OF HEYSHAM ("Railway" Magazine - 1914)

**D B McNeill**: IRISH PASSENGER STEAMSHIP SERVICES (vol 1) (1969)

**W F Nokes**: HEYSHAM HARBOUR (The Railway Magazine - Nov 1904)

**Edward Paget-Tomlinson**: THE PORT OF BARROW (Ships in Focus Record 6 – June 1998)

**A W H Pearsall**: NORTH IRISH CHANNEL SERVICES (1962)

**John Shepherd**: LIFE & TIMES OF THE STEAM PACKET (1994)

**R Sweetman & C Nimmons**: PORT OF BELFAST 1785-1985 AN HISTORICAL REVIEW

**Nick Widdows**: FERRIES OF THE BRITISH ISLES and NORTHERN EUROPE

**John de S Winser**: SHORT SEA : LONG WAR

**Manchester Central Library**
BRADSHAW'S RAILWAY AND SHIPPING GUIDES

**IOM HARBOUR COMMISSIONERS/BOARD** records held in the Manx National Heritage Library and IOM Public Record Office

**ISLE OF MAN STEAM PACKET CO** Minute Books held in the Manx National Heritage Library and Annual Reports

**SEALINK** Port Handbooks and publicity materials

*A typical summer afternoon picture of the Victoria Pier Douglas in the 1960s. (Ian Collard)*

# Appendix Two

**SHIP LIST – Vessels which have operated on Irish Sea scheduled passenger and freight services from Heysham.**

Dates of service at Heysham are indicative. Where no date is shown service may have been occasional. Where a single year is given this does not preclude the vessel having served the port in other years unless the word "only" is used. Other IOM Steam Packet vessels will have served Heysham up to 1974. Laird Lines ships often switched between routes but those listed are known to have served Heysham – although in some cases dates have not been established.

| Name whilst on Heysham services | built | operator | route | Heysham service |
|---|---|---|---|---|
| *Ailsa Princess* relief for *Manx Viking* | 1971 | Sealink-ManxLine | IOM | 1981-2 |
| *...trim* ...ld to IOMSPCo 1928 as Ramsey Town - broken up 1936 at Preston | 1904 | Midland Railway | Belfast/IOM | 1904-28 |
| *Antrim Princess* charter to Sealink Manx Line Oct 1980 & Dec 81 - also see Tynwald [6] | 1967 | Sealink-ManxLine | IOM | 1980 & 81 |
| *...alea* ...onderry/Portrush in 1905 | 1878 | Laird | | 1905 |
| *...ard* also 2002 charter to cover *Ben-my-Chree's* refit | 1979 | IOMSPCo | IOM | 1996-98 |
| *Ben-my-Chree* [6] | 1998 | IOMSPCo | IOM | 1998 onwards |
| *Ben-my-Chree* [5] only used on Heysham routes for 1985 TT races - scrapped 89 | 1966 | IOMSPCo | IOM | 1985 only |
| *Bolero* opened Seatruck Ferries route to Warrenpoint | 1985 | Seatruck | Warrenpoint | 1996 |
| *Brian Boroime* container ship | 1970 | BRB | | 1970 - 72 |
| *Brier* major fire 1917, re-named onwards *Lairdsoak* 1923, withdrawn 1933 | 1882 | Laird | Londonderry | 1905 |
| *Cambria* (3) Wartime relief in 1943 | 1921 | LMS | Belfast | 1943 only |
| *Cambria* (4) Heysham - Dun Laoghaire 1970/2 | 1949 | BRB | Dun Laoghaire | 1970 - 72 |
| *Channel Entente* Heysham - Douglas 1990 only then re-named *King Orry* [5] | 1972 | IOMSPCo | IOM | 1990 |

| Name whilst on Heysham services | built | operator | route | Heysham service |
|---|---|---|---|---|
| *City of Belfast* sold to Turkey 1925 - scrapped 1932 | 1893 | BSNC / Mid Rly | IOM | 1920 - 22 |
| *Container Enterprise* container ship | 1958 | BRB | Belfast | 1958 - 70 |
| *Container Venturer* container ship | 1958 | BRB | Belfast | 1958 - 70 |
| *Curraghmore* 1929 short charters to IOMSPCo - renamed *Duke of Abercorn* 1930 | 1919 | L&NWR / LMS | Belfast | |
| *Dalriada* also Heysham - IOM Nov/Dec 79 | 1971 | Sealink | Belfast | 1978 - 80 |
| *Dart 1* short charter to Merchant Ferries 1999 | 1984 | MF | Dublin | 1999 only |
| *Dart 1* charter to cover *Ben-my-Chree's* refit | 1984 | IOMSPCo | IOM | 2000 only |
| *Deal* cargo service Apl-Aug 1945 | 1928 | SR | Belfast | 1945 only |
| *Derwent Fisher* container service | 1966 | Sealink | Belfast | 1969 - 70 |
| *Dewsbury* wartime service - autumn 1939 | 1910 | LNER | Belfast | 1939 only |
| *Donegal* sunk by U boat 1917 | 1904 | Midland Railway | Belfast/IOM | 1904-1914 |
| *Dover* Heysham - Dun Laoghaire 1970/2. Renamed *Earl Siward* | 1965 | BRB | Dun Laoghaire | 1970 - 72 |
| *Duchess of Buccleuch* scrapped 1910 | 1888 | BSNC / Mid Rly | IOM | |
| *Duchess of Devonshire* Barrow-IOM 1897 - 1904 | 1897 | BSNC / Mid Rly | IOM | 1905 - 26 |
| *Duke of Abercorn* ex- *Curraghmore*, re-named 1930, w/d1935 | 1919 | LMS | Belfast | 1930 - 35 |
| *Duke of Argyll* (1) 1930 re-named *Alsacien* | 1909 | L&Y/LNWR | Belfast | 1923-28 |
| *Duke of Argyll* (2) war service 1939/40 and 1942/46 | 1928 | LMS | Belfast | 1928-55 |
| *Duke of Argyll* (3) burned out in Hong Kong 1995 | 1955 | BRB | Belfast | 1955-75 |
| *Duke of Connaught* (2) | 1902 | L&Y/LNWR | Belfast | 1923-28 |
| *Duke of Cornwall* sold to IOMSPCo as *Rushen Castle* - broken up 1947 in Ghent | 1898 | L&Y/LNWR | IOM | 1923-28 |

| Name whilst on Heysham services | built | operator | route | Heysham service |
|---|---|---|---|---|
| *Duke of Cumberland* 1930 re-named *Picard* | 1909 | L&Y/LNWR | Belfast | 1923-28 |
| *Duke of Lancaster* (2) war service 1939 and 1944/45 | 1928 | LMS | Belfast | 1928-55 |
| *Duke of Lancaster* (3) sold for static use at Mostyn | 1955 | BRB | Belfast | 1955-75 |
| *Duke of Rothesay* (1) war service 1939 and 1943/47 | 1928 | LMS | Belfast | 1928-55 |
| *Duke of Rothesay* (2) Heysham-Belfast 1955-67 scrapped 75 | 1955 | BRB | Belfast | 1955-67 |
| *Duke of York* (2) war service 1939/40 and 1942/47 and as HMS *Duke of Wellingtom* 1942-5 | 1935 | LMS | Belfast | 1928-55 |
| *Dunure* ex *Cedar* | 1878 | Laird | | WW1 |
| *Earl Godwin* short charter from Sealink | 1966 | Sealink-ManxLine | IOM | 1981 only |
| *European Mariner* charters Seatruck & IOMSPCo 2002 IOM | 1977 | P&O Irish Sea | Warrenpoint/ | 2002 |
| *Fern* torpedoed on route Dublin/Heysham 22.4.1918 | 1899 | Laird | Dublin | 1904-18 |
| *Hazel* sold to IOMSPCo 1919 as *Mona*. | 1907 | Laird | | to 1919 |
| *Hibernia* (3) Heysham - Dun Laoghaire 1970/2 | 1949 | BRB | Dun Laoghaire | 1970 - 72 |
| *Hoburgen* IOMSPCo charter 2004 | 1986 | Gotland | IOM | 2004 only |
| *Holyhead Ferry 1* Heysham - Dun Laoghaire 1970/2. Renamed *Earl Leofric* | 1965 | BRB | Dun Laoghaire | 1970 - 72 |
| *Hoverspeed Great Britain* | 1990 | Sea Containers | Belfast | 2001 only |
| *Irwell* wartime cargo service | 1906 | LMS | Belfast | 1941-43 |
| *King Orry* [5] sold for further service as *Moby Love 2* | 1972 | IOMSPCo | IOM | 1990-98 |
| *Lady of Mann* (1) occasional visits to Heysham in WW2 | 1930 | IOMSPCo | IOM | 1940 - 43 |
| *Lady of Mann* [2] Heysham/Liverpool - IOM | 1976 | IOMSPCo | IOM | 1985 onwards |
| *Lagan Bridge* Heysham - Belfast 1980 | 1972 | Sealink | Belfast | 1980 only |

| Name whilst on Heysham services | built | operator | route | Heysham service |
|---|---|---|---|---|
| *Lairdsbank* Heysham - Londonderry until 1930 | 1893 | Burns & Laird | Londonderry | to 1930 |
| *Lairdsbank* Heysham/Londonderry until 1963 | 1936 | Burns & Laird | Londonderry | to 1963 |
| *Lairdsglen* last Heysham/Londonderry passenger sailing (1933) scrapped 1951 | 1914 | Burns & Laird | Londonderry | to 1933 |
| *Lairdswood* | 1936 | Burns & Laird | Londonderry | |
| *Lembitu* | 1998 | NMF | Dublin | 2001 only |
| *Louth* occasional charters to LMS in WW2 | 1906 | B&I | Belfast | WW2 |
| *Londonderry* ALA Tilbury - Dunkirk route from 1930. Renamed *Flamand* | 1904 | Midland Railway | Belfast/IOM | 1904-28 |
| *Lune Bridge* Heysham - Belfast 1980 | 1972 | Sealink | Belfast | 1980 only |
| *Maidstone* Heysham-Belfast 1953-58 | 1926 | BRB | Belfast | 1953 - 58 |
| *Manx Maid* [2] withdrawn 1984 - broken up 1986 | 1962 | IOMSPCo | IOM | 1962 - 74 |
| *Manx Viking* 1985/6 charter to IOMSPC. Ex *Monte Castillo* | 1971 | Sealink-ManxLine | IOM | 1978 - 86 |
| *Manxman* then IOMSP 1920-49. Broken up at Preston in 1949. | 1904 | Mid Rly | IOM | 1905 - 14 |
| *Manxman* [2] withdrawn 1982 | 1955 | IOMSPCo | IOM | 1955 - 74 |
| *Maple* | 1914 | Laird | Dublin | 1915 - 16 |
| *Menevia* worked last LMS Heysham - IOM sailing 12.09.1927 - scrapped 1928. Ex *Scotia* | 1902 | LNWR / LMS | IOM | 1923 - 27 |
| *Merchant Bravery* 1993 Warrenpoint - 1995 Dublin - 1999 Belfast | 1978 | MF / NMF | Dublin/Belfast | 1993 onwards |
| *Merchant Brilliant* 1993 Warrenpoint - 1995 Dublin - 1999 Belfast | 1979 | MF / NMF | Dublin/Belfast | 1993 onwards |
| *Merchant Victor* later *Moondance* (Seatruck Ferries) | 1978 | MF | Warrenpoint | 1990 - 93 |
| *Merle* BFF 1996 -99 (MF Sept 2000) | 1985 | BFF | Belfast | 1996 - 2000 |
| *Mona's Isle* [5] charter 1951 then 1953 - 74 schedules - scrapped 1980 | 1951 | IOMSPCo | IOM | 1951 - 74 |

| Name whilst on Heysham services | built | operator | route | Heysham service |
|---|---|---|---|---|
| **Mona's Isle** [6]<br>former *Free Enterprise III* - reported wrecked as *Al Fahad* off Jeddah 2004. | 1966 | IOMSPCo | IOM | 1985 only |
| **Mona's Queen** [5]<br>sold for service in the Phillipines as *Mary the Queen*. | 1972 | IOMSPCo | IOM | 1985 - 90 |
| **Moondance** | 1978 | Seatruck | Warrenpoint | 1998 onwards |
| **Olive**<br>Heysham - Derry until 1930 - took last Laird Line Hey-Dub sailing 14.07.1926 | 1893 | Laird | Londonderry | to 1930 |
| **Penda**<br>Heysham - Belfast 1975 - 80 (*Peveril* from 1982) | 1971 | Sealink | Belfast | 1975 - 80 |
| **Peveril**<br>Liverpool-IOM 1981-85  Heysham -IOM 1986-98 | 1971 | IOMSPC | IOM | 1986 - 98 |
| **Peveril**<br>on charter from IOMSPCo | 1971 | BFF | Belfast | 1985 - 6 |
| **Princess Margaret**<br>sold to Far East 1962 as *Macau* | 1931 | LMS | Belfast | 1939 only |
| **Princess Maud**<br>sold Aug 1965 for Greek service as *Venus* | 1934 | LMS | Belfast | |
| **Rapide**<br>deployed on Belfast - Troon route 2003 onwards | 1996 | Sea Containers | Belfast | 2002 only |
| **Rhodri Mawr**<br>container ship | 1970 | BRB | | 1970 - 72 |
| **River Lune**<br>BFF 1993 MF 1999 | 1983 | BFF / MF / NMF | Belfast | 1993 onwards |
| **Riverdance**<br>ex- *Schiaffino* | 1979 | Seatruck | Warrenpoint | 1996 onwards |
| **Rushen Castle**<br>ex- *Duke of Cornwall* - broken up 1947 in Ghent | 1898 | IOMSPCo | IOM | 1928 - 39 |
| **Saga Moon**<br>BFF 1986 MF 1998 (lengthened 1995) | 1984 | BFF / MF / NMF | Belfast/Dublin | from 1986 |
| **Seacat Danmark**<br>re-opened Heysham - Belfast passenger service | 1991 | Sea Containers | Belfast | 1999 only |
| **Seacat Isle of Man**<br>peak summer services to supplement Ben-my-Chree | 1991 | IOMSPCo | IOM | current |
| **Selby**<br>container ship - Heysham/Belfast from 1969 to 1970 | 1958 | BRB | Belfast | 1969 - 70 |
| **Schiaffino**<br>later *Riverdance* | 1977 | BFF | Belfast | 1991 - 2 |
| **Scotia** (3)<br>sunk May 1940 | 1921 | LMS | Belfast | |

| Name whilst on Heysham services | built | operator | route | Heysham service |
|---|---|---|---|---|
| **Shamrock**<br>first Laird Line vessel to sail from Heysham (1904) | 1879 | Laird | Dublin | 1904 |
| **Slieve Bawn**<br>Heysham-Belfast cargo from 1950 | 1937 | LMS | Belfast | |
| **Slieve Bearnagh**<br>first cargo only ship built for Heysham-Belfast | 1936 | LMS | Belfast | |
| **Slieve Bloom**<br>cargo vessel | 1930 | LMS | Belfast | 1949-65 |
| **Slieve Donard** (2)<br>Heysham -Belfast relief 1964 and from 1968 | 1960 | BRB | Belfast | |
| **Snaefell** [4]<br>built as *Viper* for G&J Burns. Withdrawn 1945. Scrapped 1948. | 1906 | IOMSPCo | IOM | 1920 - 39 |
| **Spheroid** | 1971 | BFF | Belfast | 1986-2000 |
| **St David** | 1947 | Sealink | Dun Laoghaire | 1970 only |
| **Stena Sailor** | 1975 | BFF | Belfast | 1985 only |
| **SuperSeaCat Two** | 1997 | Sea Containers | Belfast | 2000 only |
| **Thistle**<br>Heysham-Dublin 1905 - broken up 1928 | 1884 | Laird | | 1905 |
| **Tynwald** [6]<br>sold for Med service as *Lauro Express* (1990) *Guiseppe D'Abundo* (2003) | 1967 | IOMSPCo | IOM | 1985 - 90 |
| **Varbola**<br>regular charters from Estonian Shipping Co | 1998 | MF/NMF | Dublin | 2000 onwards |
| **Victoria**<br>1st trip for IOMSPCo Heysham/ Douglas 23.6.1928 - broken up 1957 | 1907 | IOMSPCo | IOM | 1928 - 39 |
| **Viking III**<br>charter from Townsend Thoresen | 1965 | Sealink-ManxLine | IOM | 1980 only |
| **Viking Victory**<br>April 1981 charter from Townsend Thoresen | 1964 | Sealink-ManxLine | IOM | 1981 only |
| **Villandry**<br>1983 charter from SNCF | 1965 | Sealink-ManxLine | IOM | 1983 only |
| **Wyvern**<br>Tug/tender (pc 230) at Heysham 1905/59 | 1905 | Mid Rly / LMS | local | 1905 - 59 |

| Operators | |
|---|---|
| BSNC | Barrow Steam Navigation Co |
| IOMSPC | Isle of Man Steam Packet Co |
| BFF | Belfast Freight Ferries |
| BRB - Sealink | British Rail - Sealink |
| British Railways | |
| LMS | London Midland & Scottish Railway |
| SR | Southern Railway |
| MF | Merchant Ferries |
| NMF | NorseMerchant Ferries |
| L&Y/LNWR | Lancashire & Yorkshire / London & Northwestern Railways |